CA

LIMPENHOE
&
SOUTHWOOD

REMEMBERED

LIMITED EDITION

Sheila Hutchinson

Sheila Hutchinson

Front Cover Photograph:
The derelict Cantley Reach Mill from a painting by Stephen J. Batchelder. The date of the painting is unknown but the mill was derelict before 1900 and was eventually demolished after the sugar beet factory was built in 1912.

Back Cover Photograph:
The Cantley Village Sign, erected in 1977. It shows the 3 churches of Cantley, Limpenhoe and Southwood, a wherry on the River Yare, sugar beet, a ploughed field, a pheasant and a grebe; all symbols representing the three parishes.

CANTLEY, LIMPENHOE & SOUTHWOOD REMEMBERED

© Sheila Hutchinson 2014

ISBN 9780957462328

Published
by
Sheila & Paul Hutchinson
7, Colman Avenue,
Stoke Holy Cross,
Norwich,
Norfolk.
NR14 8NA
e-mail address:
paul.sheila844@btinternet.com

Printed
by
Really Useful Print Co. Ltd.
Bessemer Rd.
Norwich.

ACKNOWLEDGEMENTS.

I wish to express my thanks to the following people for supplying information, photographs and contributing to this book, without their help this book would not have been possible

Brian Abel, Peter Allard, Andrew Barton, Robert Beadle, Ivor & Sadie Brinded, Joy Brock, Anne & Michael Brook, Steve Cash, Jane Crossley, Christine Fisk, Brian Grint, Anne Haward, Maureen Hewitt, Rosalind Hobrough, Graham Hobrough, Alison Howes, Billy Lacey, Margaret Morton, Brenda and Paul Pawsey, Ian Redhead, Paul Rich, Maggie Risby, Ann Russell, Desmond Sharman, Pamela Tarrant, Dawn Tovell, Barbara Tuck, Bob Waters.

Disclaimer.
The information in this book has been collected from many old documents, maps, websites and people's memories. The author cannot accept responsibility for errors and omissions and apologises for any errors that may be present.
    Every effort has been made to establish copyright for the photographs used in this book. Anyone with a copyright claim is asked to contact the publisher in writing.

INTRODUCTION

I lived at Berney Arms hamlet by the River Yare from 1946 till 1963 and during that time I spent many hours sitting on the river bank watching the cargo boats, lighters, wherries and the Golden Galleon go by. Today there are only yachts, pleasure cruisers, and the odd restored wherry that goes along the Yare.

I can remember the wherry Albion sinking at Berney Arms on January 1st 1960 fully laden with sugar beet, destined for the Cantley Sugar factory, and which the men removed by a steam grab prior to the Albion being raised.

In days gone by it would have been hard work for the men working in all weathers getting the sugar beet to the factory. For many years sugar beet was delivered to Cantley on wherries or by rail but in more recent years the beet and sugar products are transported by road.

Until the turn of the last century large coasters delivered fuel to Cantley factory but the last large vessel, 'Appleby' was in about the year 2000.

Limpenhoe and Southwood are now part of Cantley Parish so they are incorporated in this book.

Cantley village on the River Yare is ten miles east from Norwich and ten miles west of Great Yarmouth. It is in the Eastern division of the County of Norfolk and was in the Blofield hundred and union. The village of Limpenhoe lies just over a mile to the north east of Cantley, and Southwood parish is about 1 ½ mile to the north of Cantley village. These too were in the Eastern division of the County of Norfolk and were in the Blofield hundred and union. Until the building of the sugar factory all three parishes were farming communities with most of the inhabitants working on the land.

Today the combined parishes are administered by Broadland District Council and are part of Brundall Ward.

CANTLEY

Today the built up area of the village of Cantley is centred in the southern part of the parish close to the railway station and the sugar factory. This was not the case till the mid to late twentieth century when considerable house building took place. Around 1900 the most 'built up' area of the village was around School Lane and other dwellings were spread across the parish. In the 1920s the Council houses were built on Church Road, and more dwellings were constructed along Church Rd in the 1950s.

The development continued during the 1960s with major house construction on Grange Road, Burnt House Road and Malthouse Lane. The rest of the parish, however, is still sparingly populated even today.

FARMING

The original separate parishes of Cantley, Limpenhoe and Southwood were, and still are, rural areas and farming and agriculture have remained an important part of life throughout the years and remain so to this day. Today, however, few people in these parishes work on the land, while a century ago most of the inhabitants worked on farms as agricultural and farm labourers, marsh men and cowmen etc.

FARMERS at CANTLEY.
Members of the Gilbert family were the Lords of the Manor and the main landowners in the parish during the eighteenth and nineteenth century and were gentleman farmers. On the Cantley tithe apportionment of 1837 William Alexander

CANTLEY, LIMPENHOE & SOUTHWOOD REMEMBERED

Gilbert owned 1,297 acres of Cantley Parish, and many of his properties had tenant farmers, so many others across the parish were listed as farmers. The following people are found in old directories and census returns listed as farmers.

Name of farmer.	Dates Listed	Notes
James Jermyn	c. 1815	
Francis Barnes	1832	
Philip Atkins	1836 - 1845	Lived at house by junction of Cow Meadow Rd & Hall Rd, area 85 on tithe map
William Burred	1836 - 1875	Lived at a cottage on School Lane, area 123 on tithe map.
William High	1836 - 1845	Occupier of the Grange & the Oaks on the tithe apportionment of 1837.
Samuel Hewitt	1836 - 1868	Occupied house on area 18 of tithe map on the High Road. (Thatch Farm).
Richard Curtis	1836 -1845	Owned cottage on School Lane, at area 124 of Tithe map.
Isaac Gown	1854 -1863	Cantley Detached by the River Bure.
Robert Howes	1854 - 1883	& publican at Cantley Cock, age 52 in 1881
William Sieley	1837 -1854	At the Ollands, area 34 on the tithe map.
James Balls	1868 - 1891	Age 58 in 1891.
Barzilla Ives	1868 - 1875	Age 40, farming 40 acres in 1871.
Henry Wright	1868 - 1890	At Olland's Farm. Age 57 in 1881.
Thomas Denny Gilbert	1871	Age 33, 992 acres, employs 35men &15 boys. At the Oaks in 1875 &1878.
Samuel Curtis	1871 - 1890	Age53, 30 acres in 1871, 100 acres in 1881.
James Sudbury	1875 - 1878	Grange Farm.
Mrs Elizabeth Burred	1881 - 1896	Marsh Farm. Age 71 in 1891, widowed. 23 acres in 1881.
Frederick Maddison	1883 - 1893	At The Oaks. & an auctioneer.
Lambert Richard Curtis	1883 - 1913	Age38 in 1891, & cattle dealer. At Marsh farm in 1904.
Thomas Allen	1883 -1890	
Robert Bloom	1890 - 1891	Age 50 in 1891. Bailiff.
William Watts	1890 - 1896	& carpenter & wheelwright. Age 40 in 1891.
Richard Wright	1890 -1896	The Cock Farm. Farmhouse located at the 'Old Cock Inn'. Age 38 in 1891.
Robert Burred	1891	Age 31 in 1891.

Barnes England	1896 -1904	& butcher, grocer, draper & overseer. Age 42 in 1901.
William Stordy Harn	1896	Manor farm.
Henry Albert Wright	1896 - 1900	The Oaks Farm.
Samuel William Curtis	1891 - 1896	Age 41 in 1891.
Benjamin Shipley Slipper	1900 - 1905	The Oaks Farm. Age 26 in 1901.
Thomas Allen	1900	Grange Farm (Fred Adams his bailiff).
William Watts	1900	Farmer & carpenter.
Thomas Kent	1905 - 1913	The Oaks Farm.
Henry Kendal Bond	1901 - 1912	Manor Farm, age 44 in 1901.(Wm. Turner was farm bailiff in 1904 & George Crowe in 1912.)
John Wigby	1904 - 1905	Grange Farm.
Benjamin A. Collins	1906 -1929	Glebe Farm.
George & Wm. Farrow	1912 -1925	Olland's Farm.
George Stephen Goodrum	1912 -1929	
Anglo Netherland Sugar Corp. Ltd.	1912	Max Martens is manager, & James W. Wright the farm Bailiff. Grange Farm.
B. S. Sillem	1916	Manor Farm, George Crow bailiff.
John Dingle	1916 - 1925	Grove Farm.
Mrs E. C. Hovell	1916	John Howlett was the farm bailiff.
Edward Karel Alexander de Neve	1922 - 1925	Grange farm. He was an agent for the Beet Sugar Corporation.
William Archer Edrich	1922 - 1925	Manor Farm.
Frank Scales	1922 - 1925	Marsh Farm.
William Walker	1922 - 1925	The Oaks.
Edward Farrow	1929 - 1937	Grove Farm.
John Thomas Farrow	1929 - 1937	The Ollands Farm.
William Ives	1937	
Fred Haag	1929 -1937	Marsh Farm, Bailiff: Ernest Read.
A. den Engelse	1937	Manager of EARP Co Ltd. The Oaks.

THE OLLANDS FARM

This is located at about TG387061.
On the tithe map this farmhouse, at area 34, was listed as owned by William Alexander Gilbert and occupied by the tenant farmer William Sieley.

In 1861 Olland House was occupied by Robert Rose an agricultural labourer age 27. Some later occupants include Fred Howard in 1894, George Myhill in 1894 &1898; William Boatwright in 1900.

In 1897 the property was conveyed to Robert Hardiment, and in 1912 & 1930 the owner was listed as Alfred Arthur Hardiment, who owned 127 acres in Cantley in 1930. It was occupied by Farrow for many years.

Olland's farmhouse, along with another cottage, 99 acres of farmland and a further 84 acres of marsh was put up for auction in September 1945. (Cubitt C. Kent £5,400) The farmhouse was a 3 bedroom, 2 storey brick and slate tile building. The farm was again put up for sale by auction in September 1964. The farmhouse by then, 1964, had mains electricity and well water.

GROVE FARM

This is located at about TG378064. No buildings were shown at this location on the Tithe Map or on the 1880s OS map. The buildings are first shown on the 1907 OS map.

THATCH FARM

This is located at about TG379060 on the east side of Manor Road.

On the Cantley tithe map and apportionment this farm property, which consisted of a house and farm buildings on area 18, was owned and occupied by Samuel Hewitt junior. He farmed here for many years.

In recent years Mr Tim Howard had the large barn converted into a dwelling in 2001, and this became the home of Jason Jenner.

THE OAKS

This is located on Burnt House Road at about TG380044 near the junction with Manor Road.

A farmhouse, and several farm buildings, was located on area 116 on the Tithe map which was owned by the Lord of the Manor, W. A. Gilbert and occupied by William High,

Some past occupants include: Thomas Denny Gilbert in the 1870s: Mrs Gilbert in the early 1880s; Frederick Maddison from about 1885 to 1893; Henry Albert Wright in the late 1890s; Benjamin Shipley Slipper in 1900; Thomas Kent in 1907: William Walker in the 1920s; H. Simon in1933; and Mr den Engelse in the later1930s and 1940s.

The property was acquired in the 1920s by the East Anglian Property Co Ltd. and used as their Estate Office, and was occupied by one of their management personnel.

Currently a business is run from the premises: Maddison & Lacey Goodman Ltd.

The Oaks Cantley.

ROPES FARM

This is located on the west side of Manor Road at aboutTG380044.
At this location on the tithe map, at area 66 is a cottage occupied by John Fulcher and on area 65 is barn and yards occupied by William High. The property was owned by the Lord of the Manor, William A. Gilbert.

On the 1880s OS map the property has more buildings here but it was not named. The name Ropes Farm first appears on the circa 1907 OS map. The buildings have altered significantly during subsequent years.

Some occupants include: Robert Muskett, 1911; William Robert Graves, 1912; Walter Dack, 1914; George Dennis Hunt occupier of the house in 1915.

Ropes Barn was sold in October1999 for £335,000, and again in July 2003 for £400,000. Mark and Jill Tingle, who run a software business, were the occupants at Ropes Barn in 2003.

MANOR HOUSE FARM

The Manor House was the home of the Gilbert family, Lords of the Manor, for many years. It is a redbrick Georgian house located at about TG380049. On the Tithe map it was located on area 53, listed as 'House, Yard, Stables etc.' and was occupied by William Alexander Gilbert, who owned 1297 acres of the parish.

The East Anglian Property Co. Ltd. eventually bought the Manor House farm farmland and the buildings. They eventually sold the house.

The large barn was used by **EARP Co. Ltd**. for a time as a pea vining station and later, in the 1960s, for grain drying and storing. Silos and driers were added in the 1980s to increase and improve the processing. Eventually, in 2008, this business was sold and **Yaregrain plc** was formed to run the grain processing.

The Manor House was for sale in October 1997 for £206,000 and again in October 2007 with a price tag of £579,000. In recent years some holiday units were added.

Some occupants of the Manor House include:

Name	Date Listed	Notes
	1768	
William Henry Gilbert	1832	
William Alexander Gilbert	1836 – 1888	Age 64 in 1871.
Henry Herbert Gilbert	1889 – 1896	Age 50 in 1891.
Henry Kendall Bond	1900 – 1912	
B. S. Sillem	1916	George Crowe bailiff
William Archer Edrich	1922 - 1925	
Frank Sidal	1940s	Owned by EARP Co. Ltd.
Mr & Mrs Robert Keating	Currently.	Aspect Global Telecoms Ltd. at the Manor House.

Postcards showing two views of the Manor House circa 1910.

MARSH FARM at TG379034

On the 1837 Tithe Map this was marked at area 192 as 'Cottage and Garden' occupied by Charles Layton and John King and the owners were the Trustees of Charles Layton. Charles Leyton was listed in 1836 as a boat owner.

The occupant here in 1854 was listed as Samuel Curtis; in 1881 the occupier was Samuel W. Curtis, a marsh-farmer of 100 acres, age 31, and in 1908 was Richard Lambert Curtis, brother of Samuel W. Curtis.

The Curtis family were responsible for the drainage of the marsh land and probably operated the Cantley West Drainage Pump. NRO/MC513/103, dated 1854, gives the cost of 8 years drainage of the marshland by, or for, Richard Curtis as £12.

In 1912 & 1915 the farm owner was listed as Edmund Roger Aliday Kerrison.

In the early1920s the farm was occupied by farmer Frank Scales, and later by Ernest Read, farm bailiff to Fred Haag.

Mr Kenneth Knights was a recent occupant.

THE GRANGE
This is located at about TG384039.

Postcard view of The Cantley Grange in the early 1900s.

This was shown on the Tithe map at area 99 as one dwelling and two outbuildings; it was owned by W.A. Gilbert and 'occupied' by William High. It is probable, however, the William High had an under tenant here as he was also listed as the occupant at the Oaks.

CANTLEY, LIMPENHOE & SOUTHWOOD REMEMBERED

On the 1880s OS map this was named as 'Cantley Grange' and appeared to consist of more buildings than on the tithe map suggesting the farm premises had been modified and extended in the years in between. By the 1920s it had become the property of the Sugar Beet factory and the East Anglian Real Property Company.

Some occupants of the Grange include: John Bales Borcham in 1868 and 1871; Mrs Anna Crocker listed in 1883 and 1896; Elizabeth Arnold in 1900 and 1902; John Wigby, a farmer in 1904; Miss Annette Marion Jane Kinder in 1911 and 1912, Eduard Karel Alexander de Neve in 1922 and 1925 and Mr Tracey Fowler in the 1930s and 1940s.

GLEBE FARM

This was located at about TG374045.

A large barn was shown on the 1837 Tithe map at area 127 but no farmhouse or dwelling was there.

Several buildings were shown here on the 1880s OS map but the farm was not named. This was first marked with the name 'Glebe Farm' on the 1907 map. Benjamin Collins farmed here for several years.

The Lacey family moved here in about 1938 and Billy Lacey was here till the late 1950s.

Most of the farm buildings were demolished in the late 1950s, and the 1970s OS map shows only Barn End near this location.

BILLY LACEY REMEMBERS

When I was a young boy I lived with my parents and two sisters on an old wherry, called the 'Fairy Queen', moored about ½ mile upstream from the Cantley sugar factory, near where the sewage works is now located. At that time there were two houses nearby, one was occupied by Fred Hollis, and there was also a wooden building called 'Bonna Vesta'. Fred Hollis along with Reggie Buck and Ernie and Geoff Read all worked for farmer Fred Haag.

From there we moved for a time to Haddiscoe, and later moved to Glebe Farm at Cantley in about 1938. I remember on my first day at Cantley school there were only four children in my class.

During the war my youngest sister and I were evacuated to Barnham Broom for a while, but I returned to Glebe Farm at Cantley when I finished school. Glebe Farm was a mixed farm with a little over 30 acres and we had use of part of the large barn next to the old rectory. The farm house at Glebe farm was, I believe, an old school building, and when we went there it had electricity laid on and we had a well.

When I returned to Cantley I worked on the farm and I was in the Home Guard. I remember the aircraft coming down on the marshes nearby, and I remember that there were Italian prisoners of war working at the sugar factory during the war years.

During my time there the post office was on School Lane, and later moved to the bottom of Church Road; Fred Burgess, who had been a marsh-man previously, ran the Falcon pub at Limpenhoe; Stanley Leman started a youth club at the village hall; and Mr Laws, who lived in a bungalow near the railway, had a market garden. Frank Sidal lived at the big house at Manor Farm which was owned by EARP Co. Ltd. and was then a poultry farm and hatchery, and Sam Mayes was a horseman at Manor Farm.

Billy Ives farmed near the Cantley Cock public house, and Billy Gladden kept cows at the bottom of School Lane. East Anglian Real Property Co. Ltd. owned Ropes Farm, Manor Farm, and Grange Farm. Mr Tracey Fowler, a manager at the Sugar Factory, lived at the Grange, and the Oaks was occupied by Mr A. den Engelse, the manager of the East Anglian Real Property Co. Ltd., while David Catchpole was a horseman at the Oaks.

Cantley Station was busy in those days. There would be three trains each day scheduled for the shift changes at the sugar factory during the sugar beet campaign; and milk churns were loaded onto the trains to be taken to Norwich each day. I got married at Cantley and lived there until the late 1950s when we moved to the marshes on the Halvergate Fleet.

ST. MARGARET CHURCH, CANTLEY

Sacred
TO THE MEMORY OF THE MEN
OF THIS PARISH WHO FELL IN
THE GREAT WAR 1914-1918

2ND LIEUT. AUGUSTUS C.H. SILLEM R.F.A.
SKIPPER ERNEST R. BROWNE R.N.R.
CORPORAL ERNEST BRINDED R. FUSILIERS
BOMBARDIER SAMUEL G. JONES R.F.A.
PTE. ARTHUR C. WOODHOUSE DUR.L.I.
PTE. HARRY R. GOLDEN M.G.C.
PTE. DAVID FUTTER NORFOLK REGT.
PTE. JOHN ABEL NORFOLK REGT.
PTE. BERTIE TURNER NORFOLK REGT.
PTE. SIDNEY G. TURNER NORFOLK REGT.

"THEIR NAME LIVETH
FOR EVERMORE"

War memorial inside St Margarets Church.

Located at TG3816704140 this Grade II listed church is built of flint with stone dressings, and lead and slate roofs. It consists of a west tower with one bell, nave, south porch, south transeptal chapel, north vestry and chancel. The tower is 14th century and the rest is 15th century. The register dates from 1559. There was a square font from the Norman period. The central priest's door has a Norman arch. Some repair work was carried out in 1844, and more restoration and re-roofing of the nave in about 1867. The chancel was restored in 1879. The interior is mainly 19th Century. There are old inscribed brasses to Frances Gaudye, died 1637, Simon Kidbull died 1735 and Jonathan Layton died 1801.

The tithes were commuted in 1838 for £308 per annum. The "Poor's Allotment" consisted of about 18 acres, awarded at the enclosure, and which was let by tender; the income from the land was distributed to the poor who did not receive parochial relief.

Some Cantley clergyman	Date
Stephen de White	1270
William Bardolf	1299
William de Corby	1306
William Avenel.	1310
Thomas de Cailly	1328
William de Bergh	1350
William de Humberston	1372
Peter de Blithe.	1373
Peter Whyten	1391
William Gilten	1398
John Cartere.	1398
John Dowes	1406
Thomas Muriel	1437
John Smith	1465
And. Jenney	1477
William Pratt	1507
Thomas Raylton	
Richard Jewel	
John Barret	1550
Greg. Madyse.	1554
William Johnson	1564
William Philips.	1584
Samuel Bramall	1603
Daniel Chapman	1639
Henry Gawdy	1650
Bernard Skelton	1663
Jeremiah. Ward	1690
Michael Hart	1695
Thomas Marlyn.	1703

John Welham.	1720
Christ Pigg	1726
Thomas Morden.	1736
John Gilbert.	1836
Robert Henry Cooper	1836
Henry Robert Gilbert	1845
R. M. Gwyn.	1845
John Denny Gilbert	1854
John Bellamy Gilbert	1860
Everett James Bishop	1893
Joseph Evans Hopkins	1900
Alfred Charles Edward Broomfield	1900
William George Rolson	1908
James William Jacobs	1930s
Edwin John Gargery	1940
Hubert Woodall Bevan	1945
Lewis Llewellyn Thomas	1951
Howard Sandrson	1955
Colin Francis Scott	1959
Ernest George Linden Ball	1962
John Adamson	1977
J. E. Hopkins	
James Frederick Headland	1981
John Handley	1986
Gibson	1994
Clive Dxbury	2002
Damon Rogers	2006

In the year 2002 the union of several benefices took place to give the united benefice of Cantley, Freethorpe, Halvergate, Tunstall, Southwood, Limpenhoe, Reedham and Wickhampton.

Two Postcard views of Cantley St. Margaret Church.

CANTLEY RECTORY

This is located at about TG375045.
On area 128 on the 1837 Tithe map, a dwelling was marked here but not listed in the Tithe Apportionment. This was the old parsonage and at that time was probably occupied by the curate Rev. Robert Henry Cooper. To the west of the dwelling was a large barn which was probably the old Tithe Barn. The 'parsonage' was listed in the 1861 census returns as 'unoccupied' and this was probably because a new rectory was about to be built adjacent to the old dwelling.

The new rectory was built in 1862 by the Lord of the Manor, William Alexander Gilbert, in an Italian architectural style and the first occupant was the Rev. John Bellamy Gilbert.

When the Cantley Benefice was united with the Limpenhoe and Southwood Benefice in 1934, the Limpenhoe rectory became the parsonage for the united benefice, and the Cantley parsonage was eventually put up for sale.

The rectory was sold in 1939 and became a private dwelling and the name was altered. It is now known as **BARN END**. It was purchased by Mr Morrish.

When Mr Morrish sold the property it was put up for offers in the region of £67,000 and was described as comprising of: *Hall, Drawing Room, Dining Room, Study, Cloakroom, Cellar, Kitchen, Utility Room, Pantry, Rear Hall, 5 Bedrooms, Bathroom, Water Closet, Two Attic Rooms, with Oil-fired central heating, mains water and electricity, outbuildings and 1.35 acres of garden. In the garden was the old Parish Room which had been converted into a garage and store-house and also had electricity and mains water connected.*

Sheepdog training by Barn End.

The present occupants at Barn End are Mr and Mrs Michael and Ann Brook. Mr Rex Smith also lived at Barn End and supervised sheepdog training courses.

The old rectory, now known as Barn End, photographed in 1971.

CANTLEY REMEMBERED 1927 – 1954 by ANNE HAWARD.

This is a look at Cantley where I spent the first 25 years of my life and where my parents Mr and Mrs Shirley Arthur Morrish continued to live until the 1980s.

The sugar factory seems to dominate the village nowadays, so let us sort that first. In the 1920s the factory was a much smaller concern and was run by the Anglo Dutch Sugar Company. The site had been chosen because of its ideal position between river and railway. Mr Morrish was an engineer and the works manager and in the 1950s when it had become part of the British Sugar Corporation, he began designing the modernization and expansion of the factory and went on to do the same for all the factories of BSC.

When I was small the village was still largely agricultural. The factory road was the only made up road once across the level crossing. Cinder roads led to the pub by the river, then called the Red House, and along past some cottages to one of the two shops, Mr Murrels, and four houses, lived in by employees of the factory like Mr Pierce the chief chemist. Two of the families were Dutch, one Canadian and Mr Pierce was Welsh. The road went on to a second and little used level crossing or turned down to the marshes past the Reads at Marsh Farm. As well as the pumping house for the marshes, there was a crazy wooden house built on the river wall lived in by an eccentric lady with faded red hair. At the other end of the village, referred to as the Top of Cantley, was the other pub, the Cock, near which was a police house and the cottage of Mr Cossey the Gamekeeper.

The village proper was on the other side of the crossing but even Church Road, where most of the houses were, was not made up. It was very broad with big

Mr Morrish, in light grey suit, with other BSC staff members outside the Red House circa 1940. Photograph supplied by Anne Haward.

patches of grass for playing on; the council houses were on one side and the private properties, mostly bungalows, on the other, and ended at the steps up into the churchyard. In a larger house by the church lived Mr Korsmit, another Dutchman and a keen gardener. Another dirt road led past the present day Half Acre Stores to

CANTLEY, LIMPENHOE & SOUTHWOOD REMEMBERED

Burnt House Road and the footpath across the fields to the other shop in the village at the bottom of School Lane. This was kept by Mr & Mrs James. She was a dear and would sometimes allow you a sample from one of the sweetie jars before you decided how to spend your Saturday tuppence. There was a tiny Post Office in a cottage next to the school and another road, Grimmers Lane, went up the hill to the Rectory. This name was supposedly corrupted from Grey Mare and the story was that smugglers used a black horse with its body coloured grey, so that in the dark it appeared headless. We all believed the lane was haunted and were anyway scared to pass the Rectory. The Revd Jacobs was something of a recluse; he cycled round the village in a flat clerical hat, muttering. He had a very small congregation and most of us attended Limpenhoe Church. When he retired early in the war, the two livings were amalgamated and Mr and Mrs Morrish bought the Rectory, thereafter known as Barn End

Cantley WI 1953 Coronation Celebrations.. Supplied by Anne Haward.

That name was in fact prophetic. A huge brick and thatch barn had stood just past the Rectory at Glebe Farm, farmed by Mr W. Lacey, who had the village milk round. Mr Hollis did the deliveries in a pony and trap. In the 1950s the East Anglian Real Property Company which had bought up most of the agricultural land in Cantley and the surrounding villages, began a policy of demolishing all the old buildings. All the old cottages went and the Glebe farm house, also the farm that stood beside the turning to Hassingham, all the very pretty cottages in Cow Meadow Road and finally the Barn itself. This would not have been allowed today.

The Manor alone escaped; it stood empty for years although the farmyard behind it was in use but no one lived in the house. The garden had gone back to nature but contained a wonderful beech tree and carpets of snowdrops; it was a great place for children to explore. In the first part of the 19th century the Manor had belonged to the Gilbert family, who built the Rectory when their son became Rector. The other large house was the Grange, where Mr Fowler, the Manager of the factory lived. There were several cottages, a farmyard and a Smithy behind it, all I believe now gone.

During the 1930s the village hall was built and provided a much needed meeting place. Due to the eccentricity of Revd Jacobs, nobody had dared make use of the Parish Room in the Rectory grounds. One of the first events held there were the 1937 Coronation celebrations, when I, attended by some other little girls, all of us suitably dressed up, was "crowned". Then all the Children had a lovely tea and we were all given mugs. Depressingly one of the next uses for the Hall was for the issue of gas masks during the Munich crisis. Mrs Morrish was far sighted enough to begin training with the Red Cross and by 1940 was qualified to set up a Red Cross Detachment in the Parish Room, now part of their property. Provided with water and electricity it became a Red Cross Point. Having a Village Hall made it possible to start a Women's Institute, also initiated by Mrs Morrish, while Mr

Edna Morrish opening the Cantley Village Sign. The bricks at the base came from demolishing Billy Gladden's outside toilet. Supplied by Anne Haward.

Morrish helped to start the tradition of village Flower Shows, one of the high lights of a Cantley summer. The Hall also provided a place for the local doctors to hold their surgery sessions, saving Cantley people from getting to Brundall or Acle.

Great changes came with the war. The First Aid Point was first used for casualties after bombs were dropped on Limpenhoe. Although several bombs fell in the parish during the time of the intensive raids on Norwich, surprisingly there was never a direct hit on the factory. There were incendiary bomb attacks and

German fighters strafed passenger trains as they crossed the marshes. The village proved most enterprising; there was a platoon of Home Guard led by Mr Morrish and Mr Leaman, the Scoutmaster, Firewatchers, an Observer Corps (based on the factory roof) as well as the Red Cross Detachment of about seven, This was assigned an Emergency Vehicle donated to the Norfolk Red Cross by the people of Lichfield, Connecticut, USA.

This van was stationed at Barn End and driven by Bob Thompson or Mrs Morrish. By this stage in the war constant sorties were being flown from US air bases in Norfolk and there were numerous crashes of planes returning from missions across the North Sea that just managed to make it to land. There was one night when several returning Liberators were shot down by a German fighter that came in with them. One of these came down in the marshes near Barn End. After a terrifying hour when we watched in horror as debris rained from above, the Home Guard and Red Cross searched the area and we took the survivors into the house. Sadly the First Aid point was used for remains. US personnel arrived and the next few days were a blur of questionings, searchings and gruesome discoveries.

There was a rumour that US servicemen who had crash landed were awarded home leave back in the States and some people put the number of crashes in the neighbourhood down to that. All of them were attended by the Emergency Van. When a Thunderbolt fighter crashed in the marshes beyond the factory - pretty well opposite the Devil's Round House, a farm on the Loddon side of the Yare, the Emergency Van was first to get near the scene and Bob Thompson and Mrs Morrish were able to get the 18 year old pilot free (he had broken both legs). He was stretchered to the Van and they took him to the US hospital. Mrs Morrish visited him as he convalesced and the two families became friends, exchanging visits and keeping in touch till he died two or three years ago aged 80.

The 1950s and 1960s brought changes of a more pleasant nature. Mrs Morrish started a Forget-me-not Club for Pensioners and I took over the Girl Guides, which had been started in response to a letter to HQ by the enterprising girls of Cantley. The Duke of Edinburgh visited to open first stages of the modernization of the factory. The fortunes of the church revived, as services were held alternately at Limpenhoe and Cantley and Guide church parades were held and Harvest Festival saw the church beautifully decorated. I was married there in 1952 and though I continued to visit frequently and keep in touch until Mr and Mrs Morrish died in 1981, I cannot chronicle all the developments since then. One exception, I do remember - the very welcome opening of Half Acre stores since the village shop at the bottom of School Lane had closed. The School also closed and many of us felt really sorry for the smaller children, who had to face a long day being taken by bus to Acle.

Anne Haward, formerly Morrish. 2013

A WARTIME NEWSPAPER CLIPPING:

"**If the enemy had ever landed (at Cantley!)**
In the early days of the war a member of the Home Guard was mounted each night on the mud filter at Cantley factory to watch for parachute landings or other items of interest. A cargo vessel lay alongside the factory and when all was quiet, except for a few planes droning overhead, one of the crew who had tarried too long at the local hostelry decided to see if his ship's Lewis gun would work. A beautiful stream of tracer bullets proved that it did.
The Corporal in charge of the guard telephoned his platoon Commander for orders. He was told to silence the man in some way or other so that Platoon Commander could finish his sleep. Appeals to the sailor met with no response. Instead the merry-maker threatened to turn the gun on the road. Further bursts followed.
After more telephoning the Platoon Commander decided to visit the factory himself. As he approached, one of the disconsolate guards heard him say to himself in despairing tones: 'Six men and they can't deal with a drunken sailor. God help us if the enemy ever lands!' Note: The Platoon Commander was Mr T.G. Fowler, general manager of the factory; the disconsolate guard was R.E. Hughes, factory accountant."

Crew of the Liberator Bomber shot down 22 April 1944.

CANTLEY FIRST AID POST.

During WWII the first aid post was located at the Parish Room next to the rectory The following is extracts from the logbook:

28-2-1943
Bombing at Limpenhoe. Casualties treated:
Mrs Jermy.... suffered from multiple cuts.
Mrs Walker ...had a broken wrist ... and shock.
Shirley Jermy ... had minor cuts.

25-3 1944
Thunderbolt crashed on river bank – pilot suffering from shock & two broken ankles. Taken in Cantley Relief Van to hospital.

22-4-1944
Liberator * bomber shot down by ME210 over Cantley – it crashed in flames at bottom of the village. 3 casualties brought to F.A.P:
Pilot: Burnt face - cut on foot & hurt ankle – shock.
Rear gunner: Burnt face - badly shot leg - compound fracture – shot in shoulder.
Waist gunner: Cut hands.
Two other members of crew taken from opposite side of river to Red House – treated by Mrs Middleton.
Four dead bodies removed.
Some casualties were taken in Cantley Relief Van to hospital.
(*Crew members: Pilot Paul T. Wilkerson – survived; Co pilot Clyde S. Sewell – fatal; Navigator Leroy A. Campbell – survived; Bombardier Richard F. Sullivan – survived; Engineer George C. Gray – fatal; RO Frank Terlesky- fatal; Asst Engineer Robert L. Dotter- fatal; RO Norman S. Reed- fatal; Gunner Henry S. Bunting – survived; Gunner Martin B. Castle - survived; Gunner James R. Murray – fatal.)

8-5-1944
Relief van out to crash at Halvergate - minor first aid to airmen.

13-7-1944
Van out to Tunstall – liberator crashed - all crew killed.

14-9-1944
Van out for 2 parachutists – one treated for shock at Barn End - other taken by Mr Preston to his home.

****

CANTLEY, LIMPENHOE & SOUTHWOOD REMEMBERED
A WARTIME POEM BY THE LATE HYLDA KAYE (GIBSON)

Not Lost - But Gone Before.

We caught the train at Cantley
On the Norwich – Yarmouth line,
The factory lay silent
For it wasn't 'beeting' time.
Within the dusty carriages
Beneath the fly-flown views
A scattering of khaki, RAF and Navy Blues
And faded tints
Of Horrocks' prints
And sturdy well worrn country shoes.

Through Buckenham and Brundall
To leafy Whitlingham
Where families by the River
Ate their sandwiches and Spam,
No bustle in the boatyards
No jet trails in the sky
No snacks on every platform of sausage rolls and pies
And on the Broads
No tourist hoards
Just reed and birds and damsel flies,

Ah Norwich! You were noble then
Though bombed and battle scarred
Your people surely striken
Ancient buildings crushed and charred
A wounded giant resting
Reviving the loam
Renewed by gentle waters and fields of poly chrome
And overhead
A silver thread
Of Liberators limping home

The train that stops at Cantley
On the Norwich – Yarmouth line
No longer grunts and puffs with steam
Her carriages are fine
The city's gaping wounds are healed
Improvements by the score
Have changed her face forever. Not lost but gone before
But in my heart
Remains a part
Of Norwich, Norfolk – '44'

****

CANTLEY SCHOOL

Cantley and Limpenhoe each had a school, but only the Cantley school now exists.

In 1870 the Forster Education Act established School Boards as an alternative to the National Schools and school attendance was made compulsory, but **Cantley** had a new National School built in 1871 at TG378045, on area 71 of the tithe map which was owned by the Lord of the Manor, William Alexander Gilbert. An earlier small parish school had existed in Cantley. The Cantley National School only had one classroom. The school was in a neglected state and repairs were carried out in 1903 and hand wash basins installed, water being obtained from an old pump. In 1906 the building was divided into two class rooms by hanging a curtain. When the Cantley Sugar Factory started being constructed in 1912 several Dutch children of the construction workers attended the school.

In 1940 electricity was installed, and mains water was laid on in 1958. School meals were started in 1949 and flush toilets were installed in 1962 when mains sewerage came to the village.

In 1959 the school became a junior only school and senior pupils attended the Acle Secondary Modern School. In 1971 a mobile unit was added for infants.

In 1983 the parents and teachers formed the Cantley School Association which organises fund raising events for the school, and in 1988 the school became a First School only.

In 1998/99 some building work was undertaken to provide an extra class, an office, a staff room and indoor toilets; and in 2007 the school became a Primary School. Cantley Primary School now has four classes and a library, and a nursery school is also carried on here.

Some School Teachers at Cantley.

Name	Dates listed	Notes
Miss Jane Curtis	1861	Age 17, schoolmistress.
Harriet Mayes	1863 - 1888	Age 25 in 1871 & living at Rectory.
Miss Martha E. Lee	1890 - 1891	Age 30 in 1891, schoolmistress.
Sarah Edith Wheeler	1896	
Miss Lucretia Mackley	1900	School mistress.
Miss Stenson	1901	
Beatrice Harwood	1904	School mistress.
Alice Lee	1911	Age 25 in 1911. Became Cadman in 1915
Irene May Megson	1922	School mistress.
Miss Adelaide P. Smith	1925	School mistress.
Miss Baxter	1930s	Head
Miss Spooner	1930s	Middle school teacher
Miss Fox	1930s	Infant teacher
Mr Mallett	1950s	Head
Mrs Wymer	1950s	Teacher
Olive Cobbett	1960s	Head
Colin Arnold	1972	Head
Maggie Risby	1970s	Teacher
Mrs Greenwood	1970s	Teacher
Mrs Marie Macfatone	1970s - 80s	Teacher
Mrs Hayley Smith	1988 - 2012	Head
Mrs Jan Pierson	2012	Head

Cantley School boys in 1967. Back row from the left: Robert Clarke, Carl Ling, Colin Forman, Richard Clarke, & Ivor Brinded.
Front Row from the left: Andrew Mace, David Farman, Christopher Daniels, & Stephen Daniels.
Photograph supplied by Ivor and Sadie Brinded.

CANTLEY, LIMPENHOE & SOUTHWOOD REMEMBERED

Cantley School photographs from early 1950s. Supplied by Maureen Hewitt.

Cantley School circa 1951. From Graham & Rosalind Hobrough.
Mr Mallett the headmaster is in the top photograph.
Roger Ditcham is the boy at the front of the lower photograph.

CANTLEY, LIMPENHOE & SOUTHWOOD REMEMBERED

ON THE RIVER YARE

Post card view from 1911 by the Red House.

The River Yare has played a big part in the history of Cantley. Until the twentieth century, when the combustion engine arrived and roads were improved, the main form of transport for large loads was by boat on the river. Wherries and other craft would have been a frequent sight on the river carrying their loads up to Norwich, and other riverside villages, from Great Yarmouth. The availability of river transport was also an important factor when the decision was made to build the Sugar factory by the riverside at Cantley.

    The river also became an attraction for sporting activities such as fishing and game shooting; and sailing became popular with the wealthy. Sailing Regattas often took place on the rivers and Cantley became one of the locations where regattas were often held in the nineteenth century. Today holiday cruisers are the main craft to be seen.

CANTLEY BOATHOUSE SITES

In 1901 when the Cantley Grange Estate was put up for sale the stretch of land to the east of the Red House Inn was put up for sale as 'boathouse sites' (NRO/PD291/28).

    Initially 35 plots were for sale, 22 of them between the Red House Inn and the east Cantley Pumping Mill, and 13 to the east of the mill. Plots 13 to 16 went to Alexander Pope of London, plot 7 to Henry Reeve Everitt of Oulton, and plots 8 & 9 to Clarkson. Both Everitt and Clarkson were members of the Norfolk and Suffolk Yacht and Sailing Clubs Association which had often had regattas on the river at Cantley. Plots 1, 2 and 6 were also sold. (NRO/PD291/29) The remaining 12 plots between the inn and the pumping mill were again put up for sale at the Royal Hotel, Norwich, by auctioneers George Fitt & Co. Ltd. on 29 June 1901. Another owner of one of the plots was William Frederick North of Norwich.

Several buildings were erected on these plots and are shown on the 1907 OS Map. Henry Reeve Everitt had a tenement erected on his plots.

Some of these plots became the Woods & Newstead boatyards. Boatbuilding yards were still marked on the 1950 OS map, long after the Sugar factory had been built, but they were removed when the sugar factory expanded.

WOODS & NEWSTEAD BOATYARDS AT CANTLEY

These were located to the east of Cantley Red House on some of the boathouse sites near to the site of the east Cantley Mill. This was listed in 1908 as Woods & Newstead 'Yacht Builders'. They built the 'Yare & Bure One Design Class' racing yachts. In the 1916 and 1922 directories Ernest Louis Woods and John Walter Newstead were both separately listed as 'yacht builders' at Cantley. Ernest Woods moved his business to Horning in 1927 and there were no boat-builders listed in the 1929 and subsequent directories.

A Peacock Series postcard, circa1904, showing a wherry alongside the Red House. On the right is the Cantley Reach East Mill, and in between the pub and the mill are buildings erected on the plots which were sold in 1901 as boathouse sites. The black buildings were the Woods and Newstead boat building yards. This area is now occupied by the Sugar Factory.

RIVER DROWNINGS

The River Yare is a dangerous place being tidal and with undercurrents. Until the late twentieth century there was much river traffic, in the early days that was wherries, and in later times large sea- going coasters coming up from Gt. Yarmouth to the Cantley Sugar Factory or up to Norwich and pleasure craft.

Over the centuries many fatalities have occurred in the river near Cantley and Limpenhoe. The following is just a few examples.

Robert Marshall, aged 64, died in 1810 when he slipped into the river near Cantley White House while he was cutting sedges.

Sarah Leeds, aged 68 in 1819 was on the wherry, 'The Farmer' travelling to Great Yarmouth when it collided with another wherry, 'The Fortitude'. The Farmer sank near Cantley White House and Sarah Leeds was drowned.

Postcard showing the Cantley Reach Mill in full sail before 1900.

From the Norfolk Chronicle 16 June 1901 is the following report:
"DROWNED WHILE BATHING AT CANTLEY.
On Monday Mr. H. E. Garrod, Coroner for the Liberty of the Duke of Norfolk, held an inquest, at the Red-house, Cantley, on the bodies of John Cooper (21) and James Lake (20), labourers, who were drowned while bathing on Sunday.

Robert Cooper, labourer, Filby, identified one body as that of Lawrence John Cooper, his son, who had lived at Southwood; and James Lake, labourer, Limpenhoe, identified the other body as that of James Lake, his son, who had lived with him until he left home on Sunday between half- past ten and eleven o'clock. His son could not swim.

George Lake, groom, Limpenhoe, said that on Sunday morning he spoke to both the deceased on the river bank, and left them there. Witness' brother said he would bathe if the other did and witness afterwards saw them taking their clothes off.

Benjamin Collins, boatman, Cantley, said that on Sunday morning he was sailing down the river Yare from Cantley Red-house, and saw some clothes on the river bank, Limpenhoe side, about 100 yards from the Round-house. There was an inlet near, where bathers often used the water.

There was a depth of 3 ft. to 4 ft., but getting towards the river there was a sudden drop to about 10 ft. or 12 ft. Witness gave an alarm to Mr. Potter and Mr. Gibbs, and they went to the spot and searched with creepers, and ultimately found the bodies of the deceased. They were both dead.

James Gibbs, of Buckenham Ferry, licensed victualler, said he went with the last witness in a boat to where some clothes were laying on the river bank. They searched with creepers, and in about two hours found the dead bodies.

The jury returned a verdict that deceased were accidentally drowned."

Riverside Villas at Cantley, believed to be the property of Henry Reeve Everitt of Oulton Broad who had buildings erected on his boathouse plots.

The new Cantley Staithe and the Reedcutters public house in 2010.
Photograph taken from the Sugar Factory by Ian Redhead.

CANTLEY STAITHE

A new Staithe was constructed in between the Reedcutters public house and the Sugar Factory. This was opened on 18th September 2010 and a charitable association was formed to control the Staithe. The project began in 2005 and received approval in 2009 when work began.

In the eighteenth and nineteenth century a Staithe was located further west along the River and was adjacent to the White House or Staithe House. That earlier Staithe was where the sewage works now stands.

CANTLEY FERRY

A ferry is marked on the 1886 and 1951 OS maps at the Red House. This was probably a 'foot ferry', i.e. a rowing boat, and was probably operated by the Red House proprietor.

A pleasure steamboat at the Red House Cantley, with Woods & Newstead boatyards, and the derelict mill in the distance. circa 1905.

Vagabond and Hustler at Cantley in December 1974.
Peter Allard collection.

CANTLEY, LIMPENHOE & SOUTHWOOD REMEMBERED

Two old postcard views of sailing on the Yare near Cantley.

CANTLEY DRAINAGE MILLS

Large areas of the parishes of Cantley and Limpenhoe near the River Yare are marsh land and have been drained for centuries. The highest point of the parish land is only about sixty feet above sea-level.

CANTLEY REACH (EAST) PUMP

This Cantley 'east' mill was marked here on the 1825 Navigation Map, but it was not marked on the 1826 Bryant's map. The mill was not marked on the 1837 Cantley Tithe Map. On the tithe map the area where the mill was marked on other maps was at the junction of areas 173, 174, 181 and 182 which were owned by William Alexander Gilbert and occupied by William High. Areas 173 and 174 were listed as 'Mill Marsh' and 'Great Mill marsh'.

A mill was, however, again marked here on the 1847 map. It is probable that the mill on the early maps became obsolete by about 1826 and was rebuilt sometime before 1847. This draining pump mill was shown on the 1880s OS map and on the 1908 OS map at about TG384034.

From a painting by Stephen J. Batchelder showing the Cantley Reach Mill without sails, date unknown. Just visible in the distance on the left, and between the two wherry's sails, are first the chimney of the Langley Steam Drainage Pump and then the Hardley drainage windmill across the Yare.

This final mill was a brick tower mill with cloth sails and drove a scoop-wheel, and is believed to have been in operation until about 1886 or soon afterwards.

The last mill here was still standing, but had no sails in 1901 when the adjacent land was put up for sale as boathouse sites; and the derelict tower of the mill was still standing when the sugar factory was being built in 1912. It was demolished soon afterwards. On the OS map circa 1928 the Cantley Sugar Factory was here and the pump was not marked.

CANTLEY (WEST) MILL

A MILL was marked at about TG376030 on Bryant's map of 1826. It was also shown on the 1825 map with the name William Henry Gilbert alongside as the landowner. The 1837 Tithe map does not show a mill here, but area 197 adjacent to the mill site was given as 'Mill Marsh' owned by William Alexander Gilbert and occupied by William High. It is possible that the windmill had become redundant before the Tithe map was drawn up.

The document NRO/Spe549.316x4, dated 3 September 1846, mentions the sale of Cantley Mills:
The highest bidder to be the buyer. Two bidders make an auction. Any dispute over the Mill to be put up again.
A deposit of 25% to be placed at the fall of the hammer. The residue of the purchase money to be paid previously to the delivery of the materials.
The mill to be taken down at the purchasers expense and removed on or before the expiration of 2 months from this date if required by the Commissioners.
Should the mill not be removed by that date, to be resold and the deficiency if any in such second sale to be made good by the defaulter at the present sale.
Purchase Price £70
Deposit £17-10s
Residue of £52-10s to be paid on 2 November.
Signatures W.A. Gilbert. John Green. John Denny Gilbert.

It is probable that this document refers to the removal of the this old drainage mill, ready for the steam pump which was built near here and was shown on the 1847 map as a 'Steam Engine'.

NRO/MC513 mentions the 'Cantley Engine', presumably located here, and indicates that it was capable of 16 horsepower and estimated that it required about 147 tons of coal for working for 153 days at 10 hours per day, over the period from March 1856 to 1857.

The 1880s OS map shows a Drainage Pump at about this location. The pump is also marked on the circa 1908, 1928 and 1950 OS maps.

CANTLEY SUGAR FACTORY

Cantley sugar factory has a special place in the history of this country's sugar industry. Built in 1912, it was the first British beet sugar factory.

For many years the beet was delivered here on wherries by river and by rail, but in more recent years the beet and sugar products are transported by road. Until the turn of the last century large coasters delivered fuel to the factory but the last large vessel was in about 2000.

Today British Sugar currently has about 750 growers supplying beet to the factory and employs a permanent workforce of about 120 rising to 180 during the processing campaign which lasts, on average, about 150 days. The factory operates 24 hours a day throughout the campaign. The factory also employs up to 150 contractors for maintenance work and to provide other services.

The factory processes in excess of 1.3 million tonnes of beet every year. On average 370 lorry loads are accepted each day. The factory can process up to 10,000 tonnes of beet a day, with an average daily throughput of 9,000 tonnes. Around 1,200 tonnes of crystal sugar are produced every day. Sugar is stored in six silos, each with a storage capacity of 10,000 tonnes. In addition to the crystal sugar, a further 30,000 tonnes of sugar is produced as a syrup which is further processed throughout the year.

Along with granulated sugar and caster, other speciality sugars are supplied for use as ingredients by the food industry. Granulated sugar is supplied in bulk and in sacks. Caster and the other speciality products are supplied in sacks. About 80,000 tonnes of sugar beet feed, a high energy animal feed in pellet form, is produced each campaign. This is sold under the Trident Feeds label.

As part of the cleaning and purification processes soil, stones and lime are recovered. Over 60,000 tonnes of LimeX45 is produced each campaign and sold to farmers to correct acidity, add nutrients, and improve the structure of the soil. Topsoil is also produced for farmers to enrich soil quality, and 7,000 tonnes of stone is cleaned and recycled as aggregate for use in the building industry. The factory can provide all its own electricity with a generating capacity of 13Mw, and any excess power is exported into the national grid.

A BRIEF HISTORY OF CANTLEY SUGAR FACTORY

The following information was kindly supplied by Steve Cash and Owen Needham.

Over a century ago in France, during Britain's naval blockade which impeded cane sugar supplies, Napoleon decreed that French farmers must grow sugar beet and encouraged the development of Sugar Beet factories. The industry which had originated in Germany spread throughout France and the Low Countries in the late

1800's but came to the UK later due to this country's naval superiority and access to West Indian sugar. However the advantages of beet in crop rotation in increasing cereal crop yield and a change to the balance of sea power brought about the conditions for the development of the industry in the UK.

In 1910 and 1911 there was much debate in the English farming community over the potential profitability of growing and refining sugar beet in this country. Encouragement was being generated by van Rossum and his colleague E.B. Ali Cohen for the crop to be adopted by English farmers so that capital could be raised for a factory, this was countered by the reluctance of growers to commit before a factory was built and they were sure of a profitable crop.

Extracts from an article in the Norwich Mercury of 11 March 1911: *"The sugar beet question yet remains an undecided question for the majority of the Norfolk farmers. As yet, it is safe to say, scarcely one of them has made up his mind whether the prospective industry is one that is going to pay or not and, till that feeling of doubt is overcome it is a moot point whether the well known stolidity of the Norfolk farmer in the face of a fresh venture can be overcome by the Dutch promoters of the scheme. At present, it must be confessed the evidence points very much the other way. Last year, it will be remembered, experimental plots were sown and cropped, somewhat late in the season it is true, but to the home farmer, accustomed to a bumper yield of mangolds, the return from sugar beet was not a very heartening one....*

......The one ray of hope that there seems to be for the Norfolk agriculturalist lies in perfecting the whole scheme within his own county by erecting a factory at the grower's own door, so to speak, and uniting the interests of both grower and sugar producer. If there is money in the industry, and he would be a very bold man who would say there was not, this seems to be the only loophole left by which the Norfolk farmer can meet the otherwise insuperable difficulty of a labour expenditure far in excess of that of his fellow farmers abroad. We see that Mr. Cohen welcomes the idea of such a crowning of the whole scheme. It is to be hoped however there will be sufficient enterprise amongst our own people to finance such an undertaking."

The driving force behind the start-up of the industry in the UK was a member of a Dutch family, long involved in the manufacture of sugar, Jan Petrus Van Rossum. Previous attempts at establishing the industry in this country had failed, through financial and technical shortcomings and the inexperience of English farmers in the cultivation of sugar beet. Van Rossum was convinced that the soil and climatic conditions of Norfolk and Suffolk, so alike those of Holland, would be ideal for growing beet. In 1910 he encouraged the support of local landowners for the venture and plans for the factory were drawn up.

Sugar beet was grown in Norfolk on a trial basis, harvested by Dutch workers and sent to Holland for processing and the quality of the beet was found to be as good as that grown in Holland. Trials had started in 1910, and in 1911 Dutch experts came over to advise Norfolk farmers on the cultivation of the crop. The beet was lifted by hand and shipped to Holland for processing.

In 1911 the **Anglo-Netherland Sugar Corporation** was registered with van Rossum as the managing director and Ferdinand Hombach as the agricultural advisor.

Cantley was chosen as the factory site because of it's proximity to the Norwich to Yarmouth railway line and to the river Yare, the major transport routes at that time. Construction began in mid March 1912 and despite floods in August 1912 and a riot the factory was completed in time for production to start on the 11th November 1912 at a cost of £170,000.

Much of the wharf and factory construction was carried out by Norwich company of J. S. Hobrough, but much of the workforce was multinational with a wide experience of the previous construction of sugar plants.

J. P. van Rossum

Virtually all the equipment was second hand from the N.V. Dordrechtshe Suikerfabrich factory in Dordrecht, Holland which ran from 1861 until 1909. The plant was shipped over from Holland and brought to Cantley by rail and sailing wherry. The new company was additionally funded by Dutch Sugar factories to the tune of £565,000 which assisted the company over the difficult first years of processing.

The factory was designed to process 800 tonnes of beet per day and on the first day they sliced 372 tonnes

From the beginning the Corporation was heavily involved in producing the crop, supplying the seed, nitrate fertiliser, labour and directing the management of the crop.

In 1912 all jobs were manual and the factory needed a total workforce of up to 600 people to be on site. In the 1913-14 campaign the factory sliced 31,800 tonnes of beet but the factory ran at a lost for many years.

Early factory construction work with the derelict Cantley Reach Mill on the right.

During WWI the lack of skilled a workforce and beet supplies caused the factory to close down in 1916, and operations were discontinued until 1919-20, when once more the factory was put back into commission. The original company was wound up and a new company '**The English Sugar Beet Corporation Limited**' was founded in 1920. Small alterations to the plant were made from time to time, but it was not until 1923 that any drastic changes took place. During that year a Steffen molasses de-sugarisation plant was put in, and this worked for two years. The Steffen process involved adding lime to molasses and subsequently recovering the sugar from the compound. It was inefficient and used huge volumes of water.

Construction workers at Cantley Factory. From Brian Grint.

However, prior to that, molasses were probably discharged to the river as a waste product. In 1924 pure Steffen was discontinued and Steffen-Diffusion was introduced. An extra cutting mill was added together with a small triple effect evaporator, a turbo alternator of 450KVA and three electric centrifugals; also a small Lime Kiln. These alterations had the effect of nearly doubling the capacity and, apart from the introduction of Imperial gas driers and one Buttner Drier, replacing steam driers, no further alterations were made until 1927.

In 1927 extensive alterations were made under the direction of Mr A. H. Friewijk. The boiler house was completely rebuilt and coal bunkers for 250 tons were also installed. In 1936 the Sugar Industry Act was passed by Parliament. It provided for the amalgamation of all existing factories into a single corporation in which the government held shares and appointed farmers representatives to the board to ensure fair pricing between growers and processors. The company was named **The British Sugar Corporation.**

In 1939 the War Agricultural Committees was set up by the government in the face of rationing with the aim of producing as much as possible. The sugar

Unloading beet at Cantley Factory in 1947. Supplied by Brian Abel.

factory produced large quantities of animal feed in the form of the dried sugar beet pulp, which was invaluable for livestock back on farms, as the sugar was to human consumers. The Norfolk farmers at that time produced about one-third of the sugar beet grown in this country.

As time progressed further alterations and expansion of the factory continued. In 1947 the factory was extended and reorganised, and in 1962 work began to build 4 sugar silos, each of which could store 10,000 tonnes of sugar. Two weigh bridges were built in 1963, pulp presses in 1965, and fuel oil storage tanks in 1968. Ponds were also built in 1968 to accommodate lime waste, and a new Dorr Effluent Thickener plant was also constructed.

Another major reconstruction took place between 1976 and 1980 to improve beet reception and handling and increase productivity, and two more silos were erected in 1980. Throughout the 1980s further developments continued and included the provision of new sugar bagging equipment, an icing sugar packing line, improved instrumentation and computerisation, and in 1988 a coal fired boiler and 11Mw turbine.

Expansion and improvements continue to this day.

DESMOND SHARMAN REMEMBERS

I left school in December 1939 looking for my first job in January 1940. I started work at BSC at Cantley in the packing plant at 12s 6d a week in old money. Many of us young boys and young women worked there at the same time packing 14 pound and 21 pound cartons in BSC paper parcels, about 30 parcels an hour.
At 15 years old I was asked if I would take on the 21 pound machine by chargehand Mr A. Talbot. I took over from Oliver Bedding who was older than me and had been called up for National Service, I think he went into the Navy. Mr Talbot was an unpredictable man but I got on quite well with him. When sirens went off

Packing sugar at Cantley Sugar Factory. Supplied byBrian Grint.

we had to shut down and go to the shelter which was just outside the No.1 warehouse. I think the management thought there was a lot of time being wasted so they brought in a crash system to warn when planes were imminent. I ran the machine till I was about 16 years old when Mr S. Wright, was over Mr Talbot, decided I would have to work loading sugar sacks on to Preston Lorries. As the war progressed most of us boys were made redundant to make room for more woman workers. Being only 16 years old I was not old enough to be called up for National Service so then moved on to other jobs. I found one working on Mr More's Farm in Tunstall

I returned to work at BSC many years later and spent another 12 years back at Cantley in No.5 warehouse before I took up a security job. When the security firm was taken over by Group 4, I was offered redundancy at the age of 64 and I accepted the offer.

MARGARET MORTON (nee KORSMIT) REMEMBERS

Frans Korsmit, a Dutchman, came to live in Cantley in 1922 to work at the Cantley Sugar Factory, after working in the sugar industry in Holland, Germany and Belgium, from the age of 18. He started working at Cantley as a chemist, but was soon promoted to shift superintendant, a post he retained until his retirement in 1957. He married his Dutch fiancé, Catherina, in 1926, and lived in Cantley, first at 'The Oaks', and then at 'Hillcrest' in Church Road.

His main hobby was gardening where he grew prized daffodils, He used to show his daffodils at the Norfolk and Norwich Horticultural Spring Show, winning prizes, and twice won a gold medal in 1953 and 1957 shows for the best bloom in the show. He also judged at various flower shows, including Freethorpe, Halvergate and Reedham. Another hobby was bowls which he enjoyed playing in the summer evenings. When he retired in 1957 he moved to live in Brundall where he called his new home 'Tamino' after his prize winning daffodil, and enjoyed his gardening until he died in 1984, aged 91.

F. C. Korsmit

Top: Cantley factory in 2009 viewed from Cantley Staithe.

Bottom: New evaporator equipment travelling by river through Reedham on way to the Cantley factory on 17th December 2013.

CANTLEY PUBLIC HOUSES

REEDCUTTERS. CANTLEY

This was show as **RED HOUSE INN** on the 1880s OS map at about TG382034. It was an alehouse and had a full licence. It was named as **RED HOUSE HOTEL** in the 1908 directory. It was renamed in about 2004 as the **REEDCUTTERS**.

It was not marked on the Cantley Tithe Map of 1837, and the area upon which it later was to appear, was then areas 183 and 185, listed as 'White House Meadow' and 'Reed Meadow', both without any buildings, owned by William Alexander Gilbert and occupied by John England junior. The Inn must have been built sometime in the late 1840s. It is probable that the pub was built some time shortly after the Norwich to Great Yarmouth Railway was constructed.

A ferry operated here and was marked on the 1880s OS map at the pub and was still marked on the 1951 OS Map.

Some owners from the licence registers include: William Alexander Gilbert, Ernest Butcher Grimmer around 1890, E. Lacon & Co Ltd from 17.08.1898, Whitbread**,** and it later became a Freehouse**.** Elizabeth Holdings are the current owners of the property

In October of 1999, after the last Cantley village shop closed, Mr Scott Ashby at the pub applied to have the summer trading shop in the adjacent outbuildings open all year round, and this was granted for a two year period. The local Post Office also moved in and officially opened at the public house on the 3rd April 2000.

Some occupants from records include the following.

Licensee or Occupant:	Notes	Date listed
.	Pub **Not** Listed.	1845
JOHN ENGLAND	age 52 in 1851 Publican & waterman: victualler at **Red House** in 1854. (Only a waterman in 1841.)	1851 & 1856
WALTER THOMAS CROWE	& wherry owner	1858 to 1880
ARTHUR JACOB GOLDSPINK	Innkeeper Age 38 in 1881	22.11.1880
JAMES WILSON	Age 33 in 1891.	19.01.1891
ABRAHAM GEORGE WRIGHT		09.03.1894
WILLIAM PETER JUNIPER		11.03.1895
BENJAMIN AMBROSE COLLINS	Age 54 in 1901.	18.11.1895
THOMAS WILLIAM PEART	& boat owner in 1908. Age 49 in 1911.	01.01.1906
JAMES BANHAM		01.01.1917

THOMAS WILLIAM PEART		19.11.1917
EDWARD HENRY HAMMOND		07.11.1927
JAMES JENNINGS		26.04.1937
BERT NELSON		11.04.1950
FREDERICK WARMAN		20.09.1954
HAROLD MARSHAL LOWE		10.11.1958
EDWIN JAMES CORNELIUS JONES		23.05.1960
EDWIN CHARLES GRAVES		04.06.1962
MARJORIE PHYLLIS GRAVES		14.01.1963
DAVID FUTTER &GARY BURR		1970s
SCOTT ASHBY	Ran post office here.	c. 2000.
MICK COTTRELL& PHIL CRONIN		c. 2004
PETER & LISA MORRIS		2012

Cantley Red House. Photograph supplied by Maureen Hewitt.

WHITE HOUSE: CANTLEY.

It is possible that another earlier public house was located on the riverside to the southwest of the Reedcutters. This was shown on the 1826 Bryant's Map at about TG379033 as the **White House**. This was also shown on the earlier Faden's 1797 map but as the '**STAITHE HOUSE**'.

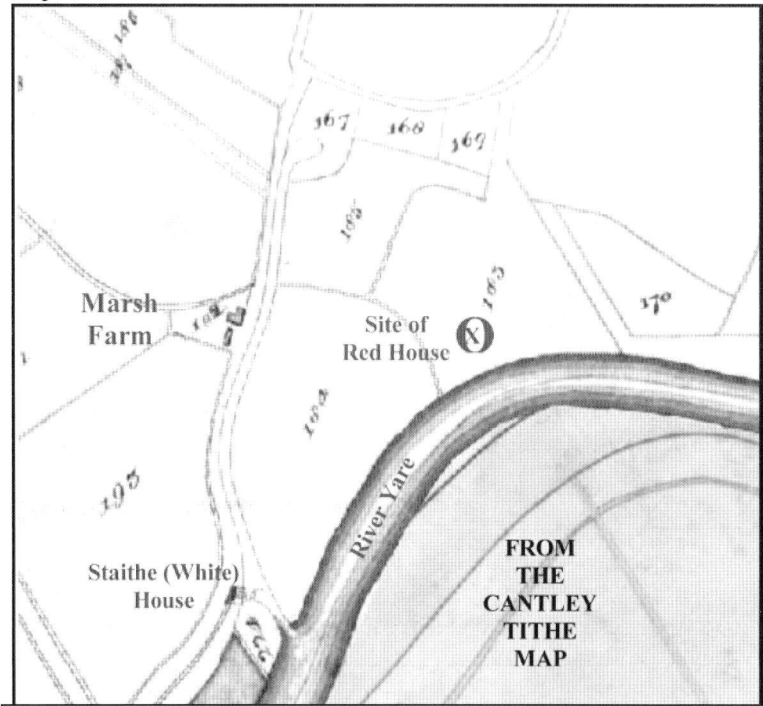

Tithe Map showing the location of the White House and the site where the Red House was later built.

The Norfolk Chronicle of 29th April 1820 carried an advert:-
'Cantley WHITE HOUSE - Situated on river, half way between Norwich and Yarmouth, with the Staithe thereto belonging............ An excellent meadow of 6A 0R 14P with the Common Allotment included............ a most desirable property situated for Brewers, Malsters and the Corn Trade - Apply to Mr Samuel Mitchell, land agent, Norwich'

The Norfolk Chronicle of 22nd July 1820 reported on a theft of coals from the wherry 'Accommodation' moored at the White House at Cantley on 10th May 1820. The coals were put into a bin owned by Edward Layton, proprietor of the White House.

CANTLEY, LIMPENHOE & SOUTHWOOD REMEMBERED

The 1837 Cantley Tithe map shows at area 225 'Cottage & Garden' owned and occupied by John England senior. This was at the location of the White House, but it was not named or listed in the Apportionment as a public house. This area is now the location of the local sewage works.

The 1847 map also shows 'Cantley White House, Stables & Garden', near the river, with owner William Alexander Gilbert and the occupier as John England junior, but no evidence of it being a public house at that time is available. Buildings at this location were marked on later OS maps through to about 1950, but were never named. The Staithe also remained here and other buildings, including a boathouse, were shown nearby on later OS maps until the **Sewage Works** was built at this location and was shown on the 1972 OS map.

CANTLEY COCK TAVERN

This is located at about TG380058 on Manor Road at the junction with Norwich Road. In 1837, on the Cantley Tithe map, the buildings at this location, area 45a, were recorded as owned and occupied by William Stout, and were listed as a **'house and shop'**, and **not** a public house.

The public house at that time (1837) was located at about TG380056 on the east side of Manor Road, on area 47 of the Tithe Map, and was owned by William Alexander Gilbert and occupied by William Sieley, and was listed as **'Cock Public House'**. The 1880s OS map also shows at this location 'Cantley Cock Public House'.

Sometime around 1890 the pub moved to its current location and on the 1907 OS map the Cantley Cock is shown at its present position, and the 'Old Cock Inn', now a farmhouse, was occupied in 1894 by Richard Wright, and in 1901 and 1911 by Samuel William Curtis.

Some owners of the pub include: W A Gilbert**,** Steward, Patteson & Finch after 1875, then Steward & Patteson till February 1967. It was then Watney Man, who closed the pub on 21 October 1975. It was later reopened, in 1976, as a Freehouse.

Some occupants from records include the following.

Licensee / Occupant	Dates Listed	Notes
ROBERT NICHOLLS	1789 - 1794	
WILLIAM SIELEY	1836 - 1841	age 50 in 1841.
AMOS REYNOLDS	1845 - 1865	age 46 in 1851 & farmer.
HENRY WRIGHT	1869 - 1872	& farmer, Age 49 in 1871
ROBERT HOWES	1872 - 1884	age 52 in 1881.
JAMES THIRKETTLE	17.11.1884	
GEORGE WILLIAM RALLING	15.11.1886	
RICHARD DAVISON	21.01.1887	
WILLIAM EDGAR LINCOLN	21.01.1889	age 63 in 1891.
WILLIAM BARNEY	09.11.1891	age 60 in 1901.

CANTLEY, LIMPENHOE & SOUTHWOOD REMEMBERED

ARTHUR ROBERT SYMONDS.	09.11.1903	Age 44 in 1911.
WALTER WILLIAM GOLDEN	06.04.1914	
WALTER ALAN PEART	14.02.1927	
WALLACE G BROWNE	13.01.1930	
FREDERICK GEORGE KNIGHTS	27.11.1933	
HAROLD J GARDNER	24.06.1935	
ALICE MARY GARDNER	03.06.1952	
WALTER GEORGE SHORTEN	20.10.1952	
RAYMOND CHARLES PALMER	26.07.1954	
FRANK MANDERS	07.03.1955	
ANN MANDERS	28.01.1959	
FRANK BENJAMIN BRISTER	12.02.1962	
M. ENRIGHT	Currently	

Cantley Cock in 1901. The name above the door is William Barney.

52

CANTLEY SHOPS

On the Tithe map of circa 1837 Mary Smith and John Gower occupied area 73, listed as a cottage. This was on School Lane and to the west of the present school where Highfield later appeared. This was the village shop at that time, as Mary Smith was listed as a shopkeeper.

At the location 45a on the tithe, now the Cock public house, another shop was listed in 1837 but this may only have been a blacksmith's shop.

The shop moved to the other end of School Lane and later became known as the 'Stores'. This was at area 123 of the tithe map

The last shop closed in 1999 but a shop was opened at the Red House

SOME CANTLEY SHOPKEEPERS

Name	Dates Listed	Notes
Mary Smith	1836 & 1845	Area 73 on tithe map.
William England	1861 - 1891	&butcher, & carrier in 1883. Age 62 in 1891 on Marsh Road at area 123 of tithe map
Mrs Susan England	1892	& butcher. Wife of William.
Barnes England	1904 - 1909	Son of William England. & butcher, farmer & draper.
Arthur George Thompson	1911 & 1925	Age 38 in 1911.
Herbert William Murrell	1933 - 1937	General stores, boot repairer, newsagent & cycle agent, shop known as Rusticana.
William Henry James	1933 - 1951	Grocer on School Lane
Mr & Mrs Hobrough	1951	School Lane & Post Office

ROSALIND AND GRAHAM HOBROUGH REMEMBER CANTLEY

Our parents, Arthur and Mary Hobrough, moved to Cantley in August 1951 to run the Post Office (mother was the sub-postmistress) and the Village Stores on School Lane. The previous sub postmaster was Mr. James.

Our father was sometime School Manager, Clerk to Parish Council and may have been on the Village Hall Committee. For a time he belonged to the Bowls Club.

Our mother was sometime member of the Parochial Church Council and member of the St Margaret's Church choir. She took over the 1st Cantley Guide Company from Ann Morrish, whose parents lived at Barn End, which was the Rectory at one time. The Company then met in the Parish Room there. This would have been 1952 or early 1953. In 1953 our mother started the Brownie Pack. Brownies and Guide meetings were held in the Village Hall. She later started a non-denominational Sunday School held in the Village Hall. She gave up the Post office in 1969. The shop continued until May 1973, when, on retirement, they moved away from the village.

On Coronation Day, June 2nd 1953, games were held alongside the big barn near the Village Hall. There was a Fancy Dress competition for children. The weather on the Coronation celebration day was poor and we remember taking cover in the glasshouses near the barn. The profits from the events went towards the children's play swings which were put up in the grounds of the village hall.

At one time the County Library stored books in a cupboard in the large classroom of the School and once a fortnight, after school hours, Mrs Carter and Mrs Catchpole of the village, used to issue books to villagers.

Mr Mallett, the school master lived at Halvergate near the old corn mill and cycled to Cantley School each day. Mr Newstead lived at the other end of School Lane where the earlier post office had been located

The 1953 Coronation celebrations. Fancy dress competition in the glasshouse near the barn. Supplied by Rosalind and Graham Hobrough.

1953 Coronation celebrations. Supplied by Rosalind and Graham Hobrough.

1953 Coronation celebrations. Supplied by Rosalind & Graham Hobrough,

POST OFFICES

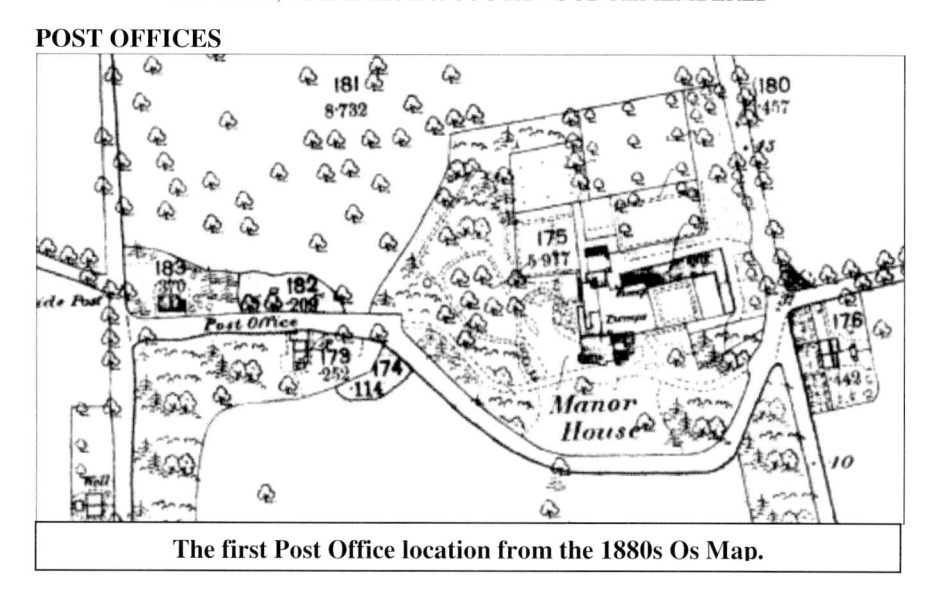

The first Post Office location from the 1880s Os Map.

The first Cantley Post Office was located on Cow Meadow Road close to the Manor House and was marked on the 1880s OS map. This was area 80 on the Tithe map of circa1837, listed then as cottage occupied by Philip Wingfield and owned by W. A. Gilbert. It became a post office in the 1850s.

Before the 1907 OS map was drawn the post office had moved to School Lane between the Smithy and the Cantley School. The post office later moved to the other end of School Lane near the junction with Grimmer Lane.
The post office was once again moved to Malthouse Lane, and in 2000 a post office was run from the Cantley Red House public house by the river.

The 1900 directory gives the following information: *"Thomas Sales sub-postmaster. Letters through Norwich arrive at 8:35 am, 2:30pm & 5pm; dispatched at 12:55 & 5:55pm. Sunday arrive at 9am, dispatched at 10:30am. Postal Orders issued here but not paid. Freethorpe is nearest MO office, telegraph office is at Railway Station for collection & Reedham for delivery of telegrams. Pillar letter box Manor corner cleared at 5:55pm & 10:45 Sundays. Wall letter box at Railway Station cleared at 1:20 & 6:20pm October to June; 6:10pm July to September weekdays."*

Some postmasters from records include the following:

Name of Sub- postmaster	Dates Listed	Notes
John Crane	1854	
James Brett	1861	Age 60. Footman in 1851.
Mrs Brett	1863	
John Harper	1868 - 1896	age 40, in 1871. Listed as a gardener in 1871 & 1891.

Thomas Sales	1900	& blacksmith
Harriet Sales	1904 -1912	Age 59 in 1911. (wife of Thomas Sales, the blacksmith)
John Walter Newstead	1916 - 1937	& stationer (& yacht builder).
William Henry James	1937 - 1951	
Mrs Mary Hobrough	1951 -1969	
Scott Ashby	2000	At the Red House.

The building which became the third Cantley Post Office, located at the end of School Lane. From Graham and Rosalind Hobrough

The 1937 directory says that Eliot Blake, physician, attends at the post office on Mondays and Fridays between 11 and 12 o'clock. Doctor Blake travelled to the village from the Reedham surgery.

BLACKSMITHS

The blacksmith's shop at Cantley was located on School Lane. It was shown as a 'cottage and blacksmith's shop' on area 74 of the Cantley Tithe Map, owned by W.A. Gilbert and occupied by William Thirkettle and William Marshall. The owner of this property in 1912 was listed as Walter Robert Sales of Norwich. The blacksmith's shop was marked on the 1907 OS map but was not indicated on the 1927 map suggesting the smithy had closed between those years.

It is possible that another blacksmith's shop existed at the current location of the Cock public house, i.e. on area 45a of the Tithe map, as this was listed in 1837 as a shop occupied by William Stout who was a blacksmith.

Another smithy also once existed at the Grange in later years.

Name	Dates listed	Notes
William Stout	1836 - 1854	Age 50 in 1841.
William Thirkettle	1836 - 1854	Age 34 in 1851
William Bulley	1861	Age 37i n 1861.
David Tills	1861- 1868	Age 31 in 1861.
Benjamin Wyant	1871 - 1878	Age 27 in 1871.
William George King	1881 - 1883	Age 29 in 1881, & carpenter & wheelwright.
George High	1891	Age 17, apprentice.
Thomas Sales	1890 - 1912	& agricultural implement maker. Age 37 in 1891.

POLICE

The old Cantley police house is located on the east of Manor Road and to the south of the Cantley Cock public house. This current house was built in the 1950s. Prior to the building of the new police house the village had a police constable who resided elsewhere in the village.

Some constables from the directories are listed below.

Name	Date listed	Notes
John Riches	1847	Policeman.
Francis Brown	1854	Parish Constable.
William Claxton	1861 - 1871	Age 55 in 1871 Police constable. Later listed as Parish Clerk
Nathaniel Hammond	1890 - 1893	Police Constable, age 42 in 1891 living near the Cock Inn.
William Mackerell	1912	Police Constable.
George Hunt	1916 - 1925	Police Constable.

The old police house was up for sale in 2004 for £98,000

RAILWAY

The Yarmouth and Norwich Railway was the first railway in Norfolk following an act of Parliament in June 1842.which authorised the issue of £200, 000 worth of shares for the construction. The chief engineer was Robert Stephenson and the chairman George Stephenson. Peto and Grissell were awarded the construction contract. Construction began the following year and the line was opened in ceremonial fashion on 30th April 1844. A station was built at Cantley and opened on 1st May 1844 for the first passenger service.

Cantley Station Staff circa 1920. Supplied by Joy Brock.

The railway later became the Great Eastern Railway in 1862 and eventually L.N.E.R. It is now part of the Wherry Lines.
Railway sidings were provided alongside the sugar factory for many years.
The Cantley station closed for freight on the 6th March 1967.

CANTLEY STATION MASTERS
The following were listed in old directories and in census returns.

Name	Date listed	Notes
John Reeve	1854	
Robert Durrant	1861	Age 31 in 1861.
William Harling?	1863	
Thomas Harding	1868 - 1878	Age 39 in 1871
William Belton	1879 - 1883	Age 40 in 1881
Walter Collins	1885 - 1893	Age 52 in 1891
Henry Jackson	1895 – 1910	

Ernest William Marshall	1911 - 1913	Age 45 in 1911.
Thomas Arthur Saward	1915	
Henry Avery	1916	
James Henry Crosby	1922	
John Payne	1925	
G. E. Taylor	1930s	

Friends of Cantley Station known as FOCUS was started in October of 2007 with the aim of enhancing the station and obtained limited funds from Wherry Lines, the parish council and from Membership contributions. Work began the following year to clean up the station and plant flower beds. The group meets twice a week.

First railway time table. Supplied by Andrew Barton

Two postcard views of the crossing and signal box at Cantley Station. Supplied by Paul Rich and Brian Abel.

Mr & Mrs Thompson and son Keith at Cantley Station in 1953. Mr Thompson worked at Cantley factory for 31years from 1922 before emigrating to New Zealand. Supplied by Joy Brock.

CANTLEY VILLAGE HALL

The Cantley village hall is a metal building located on Manor Road to the east of The Oaks. Prior to the erection of the village hall the parish room near the Rectory was used for committee meetings, the 'Forget Me Not Club' and the girl guides meetings.

The Cantley residents had for some time been collecting funds for a village hall, when in November 1931 Joannes Petrus Van Rossum presented a plot of land of one acre as a site for the Cantley Village Hall.

The plot was part of the farmland then known as the Manor and Grange Farms which J.P. Van Rossum had purchased in 1926 from Antonius Johannes Ignatius Maria Smits.

A contract was drawn up between Van Rossum and Henry William Jackson, Alfred Barker Youngs and Walter Alan Peart as trustees for the transfer of the land. The management and control of the village hall, and the erection, construction, maintenance and furnishing was to be vested in an elective committee to consist of 7 Cantley residents. The plot of land conveyed to be used in perpetuity as the village hall as a reading room and club for the use of all persons of the age of 16 years and upwards resident in the village or within a radius of six miles.

The first seven committee members were the 3 trustees. Henry William Jackson, Walter Alan Peart and Alfred Barker Youngs along with Arthur Shirley

Morrish, Charles William Sewell Vicars, Mrs Dinah Futter, and Mrs Mary Ann Jones.

Today the parish council hold some of their meetings here and the toddlers come here for the "Cantley Tots Stay & Play".

CANTLEY BOWLS CLUB

This is located near Station Road and was established in 1935 by British Sugar.

MAUREEN HEWITT REMEMBERS

I spent the first 3 ½ years of my married life living in Cantley. My two daughters were born at number 2, Windsor Road. In 1966 I moved to Moulton St Mary. A few years later Jackie and Janette started Sunday School at Cantley, and they became brownies with the 1st Cantley Brownie Pack.

Tree planting. On the left is Tawney Owl Frances Duncan, Valerie Pugh nee Jermy, brownie Stephanie Shingles and Miss Sharman. From Maureen Hewitt.

I helped to taxi the brownies to revels, thinking day services and outings etc. and after a while I helped at the weekly meetings which were on a Monday evening 6.15 to 7.30.

CANTLEY, LIMPENHOE & SOUTHWOOD REMEMBERED

When Brown Owl, Mrs Hobrough, was going to retire I was asked if I would consider becoming Tawny Owl. After much discussion I said yes. Mrs Sharman was now Brown Owl, I was Tawny and Frances Duncan came in as helper.

Everything was going fine; well that was until Brown Owl said she would like to retire next July. So in September I became Brown Owl and Frances Duncan was enrolled and became Tawny Owl. Later Joan Wallace joined.

Corrina Frost was the first brownie I enrolled; I'm not sure who was the more nervous. Nearly the last brownie I enrolled was my granddaughter Michelle Foreman.

After twenty years being involved with the brownie pack it was now time for me, and Tawny Owl, to retire. Thanks to a wonderful group of parents, they gave us a retiring send-off that will never be forgotten.

I remember three special events:

The planting of a tree to celebrate the years of Cantley Brownies.

Fund raising to buy a lectern for St Margaret's Church to celebrate the Queens Silver Jubilee in 1977 and a service of dedication being held by the Bishop of Norwich.

The pack coming runner up in the Norfolk Road Safety Quiz.

Brownies in 1991. The four with the winners trophies are Alice Milner, Anna, Wade, Hannah Jane Pawsey and Paula Soames. Supplied by Maureen Hewitt.

65

CANTLEY & DISTRICT WOMEN'S INSTITUTE.

This was established in 1939 and held meetings at the Cantley village hall on the third Wednesday of each month. They organised trips around the region and celebrations.

Cantley W.I. members circa 1940s. Supplied by Maureen Hewitt.

THE LATE CAROLINE MASSINGHAM, NEE FIELD.

Born in 1905 she lived at Cantley and recalled that the families living near the school were Youngs, Newstead and Jones, and the Collins family lived in the farmhouse near the rectory. There were less than fifty children attending the school when she was a pupil. The Manor and most of the land belonged to Mr Sillem, and in the Manor gardens were unusual fruit trees such as mulberry, quince and medlars. They used to walk through the manor gardens to fetch milk and there was a lot of noisy peafowl and peacocks.

She recalled the 1918 flu epidemic: "My brother and I went to the shop. It was closed and not a single person anywhere – no letters were delivered – the butcher, baker etc did not call – it was several days before people began to come out. My mother and us four children were all in bed for some days – we did not feel hungry just terribly thirsty".

CANTLEY, LIMPENHOE & SOUTHWOOD REMEMBERED

CANTLEY OCCUPATIONS FROM CENSUS RETURNS

The following table shows the number of people with the stated occupations and shows that the largest percentage worked on the land.

1861		1871		1891	
Agricultural Lab	46	Annuitant	3	Agricultural Lab	16
Blacksmith	3	Blacksmith	1	Army Major	1
Coachman	1	Coachman	1	Assistant	2
Cook	1	Cook	2	Assistant Grocer	1
Dairymaid	2	Dressmaker	1	Auctioneer	1
Dressmaker	1	Engine Driver	1	Auctioneer/farmer	1
Farmer	3	Farmer	4	Blacksmith	2
Farmer/Innkeeper	1	Farm Bailiff	2	Coachman	1
Farm Bailiff	2	Fisherman	1	Cook	2
Gardener	1	Gardener	2	Cowman	1
Groom	1	Groom	1	Domestic Servant	11
Housemaid	3	Housemaid	3	Dressmaker	2
Housekeeper	5	Labourer	41	Engine driver	1
House servant	1	Laundress	1	Farmer	7
Innkeeper	1	Marsh Farmer	3	Farmers son	1
Independent	2	Office Co. Reg.	1	Farm Bailiff	1
Magistrate/Land Prop	1	Police Constable	1	Farm labourer	13
Mash farmer	2	Publican	1	Farm Steward	1
Marsh man	1	Publican/farmer	1	Fisherman	1
Pauper	1	Physician	1	Gardner	2
Plate layer	1	Rector	1	Grocer	1
Police constable	1	Servant	7	Groom/ gardener	1
Railway Lab	2	School Mistress	1	Housekeeper	1
Rector	1	Shepherd	2	Labourer	3
School mistress	1	Shopkeeper/Butcher	1	Marsh man	2
Seamstress	1	Station Master	1	Police Constable	1
Servant	2	Tailor	1	Postman	1
Shepherd	1	Undergraduate	1	Publican	2
Shopkeeper	1	Waterman	1	Railway Labourer	2
Shop hand boy	1			Railway Platelayer	1
Sub Post Master	1			Railway Signalman	1
Station Master	1			School Mistress	1
Tailor	1			Stable boy / groom	1
				Station Master	1
				Wheelwright	3

CANTLEY SURNAMES FROM CENSUS RETURNS

1861	1871	1881	1891
ALDOUS	BALLS	ADAMS	ADAMES
ALGATE	BARBER	ALGATE	ALDERTON
AVERSON	BAYFIELD	ANTON	BALDWIN
BALLS	BENSLEY	BALLS	BALLS
BARBER	BETTS	BANHAM	BLOOM
BEALRIGHT?	BOAST	BARBER	BROOK
BRETT	BORCHAM	BELTON	BROWN
BROOM	BROWN	BLOOM	BURRED
BROWN	BURRED	BRINDED	CHITTLEBURGH
BUCKINGHAM	CLAXTON	BROWN	CLAXTON
BULLEY	CROW	BULLEY	COLLINS
BURGESS	CURTIS	BURRED	COOPER
CHILDERS	DANIELS	BURWOOD	CROKER
CLAXTON	DAY	CLAXTON	CURTIS
CROWE	DINGLE	CROCKER	DAGLESS
CURTIS	DUNT	CURTIS	DANIELS
DANN	ELINGHAM	DANIELS	DAY
DAYDUNT	ENGLAND	DAY	DEWING
DURRANT	ETHERIDGE	DINGLE	DUNT
ENGLAND	FULCHER	DUNT	DOER?
ETHERIDGE	GILBERT	ELLINGHAM	ENGLAND
EWLES	GOFFIN	ENGLAND	ETHERIDGE
FRANCIS	GOODRUM	FISKE	FULCHER
FULCHER	GOWEN?	FORDER	FUTTER
GARRARD	HALL	FOULGER	GILBERT
GARWOOD	HARDING	FULCHER	GODFREY
GILBERT	HARPER	FUTTER	GOODRUM
GOULD	IVES	GILBERT	GOODSON
GOWER?	KILLINGTON	GIMBLE	GUNNS
GOWEN?	LAKE	GOLDSPINK	HAMMOND
HALL	MALE	GOODRUM	HARPER
HARPER	MAYS	HABY	HARWIN
HOFFER	MORE	HALLS	HIGH
HOOTE	MUNFORD	HARPER	HOWES
HOWARD	NICHOLLS	HOLLAND	HUBBARD
KING	RAVEN	HOLLIS	HURN
LIFFAGE?	ROBINSON	HOWES	JACKSON
LITTLEWOOD	ROSE	HUNT	JARY
MARKHAM	RUDLING?	JACKSON	KEY
MOORE	RUDRUM	KING	LEA
MUNFORD	SAMPSON	LAWES	LEVERINGTON
NICKOLLS	SHEARING	MAYES	LINCOLN
PERT?	SHREEVE	MOLL	MADDISON
RENNOLDS	SCOTT	MOSS	MUNFORD
RICHES	SMITH	MUNFORD	NEWSON
RIGHT	STEWARD	OAKLEY	OLDMAN

ROSE	THAXTER	PALMER	RAYNER
RUDRUM	TURNER	RAYNER	ROSE
SAUNDERS	VERMONT	ROSE	SALES
SCOTT	WILSON	RUDRUM	SEAMAN
SHEARING	WEBB	SEAMAN	SCARLETT
SHREEVE	WOODS	SHAWRY	SCOTT
SMITH	WRIGHT	SHORTON	SHEARING
STEWARD	WYANT	SHREEVE	SHREEVE
STOUT		SMITH	SHORTEN
TILLS		SMITHSON	SMITH
TURNER		SPINKS	SWANN
WARD		STUBBS	TAPPLY
WATERS		THAXTER	THAXTER
WILSON		TRETT	TINGLE
WOODS		TURNER	TURNER
		WARD	WATTS
		WIBBLE	WEBB
		WILSON	WILSON
		WOODS	WOODHOUSE
		WRIGHT	WRIGHT

1912 REGISTERED VOTERS FOR CANTLEY

Those marked with * in the final colmn are not resident in the parish.

Surname	First Names	Qualifying Property location	
ABLE	FRANK	SOUTHWOOD RD	
ADAMS	ROBERT	BY GRANGE	
ALLEN	THOMAS HENRY	BY RAILWAY STATION	
ATTOE	GEORGE	BY SHOP	
BALLS	JAMES	BEIGHTON RD	
BARBER	EDWARD	BY COCK INN	
BIOND	HENRY KENDALL	CANTLEY MANOR ESTATE	
BRINDED	HERBERT	BY RAILWAY	
BRINDED	WILLIAM	BY RAILWAY	
BROWNE	EPHRAIM	BY MANOR HOUSE	
BROWNE	ERNEST ROBERT	BY RAILWAY	
BROWNE	GEORGE	BY RAILWAY	
BROWNE	THOMAS	THE SPONG	
CADMAN	JANE	STATION ROAD	
CLAXTON	FREDERICK	IN THE STREET	
COLLINS	BENJAMIN AMBROSE	GLEBE FARM	
CROXTON	SAMUEL	HASSINGHAM RD	
CURTIS	LAMBERT RICHARD	BY RAILWAY	
CURTIS	WILLIAM	BY COCK INN	
CUSHION	WILLIAM	SCHOOL LANE	*
DINGLE	JOHN	BEIGHTON RD	
ECCLESTON	THOMAS	BY RIVER	
EVERITT	HENRY REEVE	BY RIVER	*

CANTLEY, LIMPENHOE & SOUTHWOOD REMEMBERED

FARROW	GEORGE	OLLAND'S FARM	
FARROW	WILLIAM	OLLAND'S FARM	
FORDER	HORACE	HASSINGHAM RD	
FUTTER	FREDERICK	BY COCK INN	
FUTTER	JAMES	BY RAILWAY	
GILBERT	HERBERT HENRY	BY RAILWAY	*
GOODRUM	GEORGE STEPHEN	BY COCK INN	
GOODWIN	ANNA	STATION RD	
GREAVES	WILLIAM ROBERT	ROPE'S FARM	
HANTON	MAJOR	BY RAILWAY	
HARDIMENT	ALFRED ARTHUR	OLLAND'S FARM	*
HOLMES	FREDERICK	STATION RD	
JACKSON	JAMES	BEIGHTON RD	
JONES	SAMUEL GEORGE	SCHOOL LANE	
KENT	THOMAS	OAKS FARM	
KERRISON	EDMUND R.A.	MARSH FARM	*
KIDMAN	SAMUEL HEWITT R.	BEIGHTON RD	*
KINDER	ANNETTE MARION JANE	THE GRANGE	
LOADES	CHARLES	NEAR RECTORY	
LOADES	JAMES	NEAR RECTORY	
MARSHALL	ERNEST WILLIAM	RAILWAY STATION	
MOORE	WILLIAM	BY RIVER	*
MUSKETT	ROBERT	OLLAND'S FARM	
NEWSTEAD	JOHN WALTER	THE STREET	
NORTH	WILLIAM FREDERICK	BY RIVER	*
PEART	THOMAS WILLIAM	RED HOUSE	
POPE	ALEXANDER	BY RIVER	*
READ	STEPHEN GOOCH	MARSHES	*
ROLSTON	WILLIAM GEORGE	THE RECTORY	*
ROSE	HENRY	BY RAILWAY	
ROSE	WILLIAM	BY MANOR HOUSE	
RUDRUM	ARTHU	BY MANOR HOUSE	
SADD	HENRY EDWARD	MARSHES	*
SALES	THOMAS	THE STREET	
SALES	WALTER ROBERT	SCHOOL LANE	*
SHORTEN	THOMAS	BY RIVER	
SYMONDS	ARTHUR	COCK INN	
TOWLER	RICHARD THOMAS	RIVERSIDE COTTAGE	*
TURNER	ROBERT	BY SPONG	
TURNER	WILLIAM	BY RAILWAY STATION	
WATTS	ALBERT	THE STREET	
WHATLING	ALLEN	BY OAKS FARM	
WILKINSON	PHINEAS	NEAR STATION	*
WOODS	ERNEST	BY RAILWAY STATION	
WRIGHT	RICHARD	BY RAILWAY & MILL DYKE	
YOUNGS	ALBERT BARKER	BEIGHTON	

CANTLEY DETACHED.

Until the Norfolk Review of 1935 an area next to the River Bure was part of the parish of Cantley and was known as Cantley Detached. This area is now part of Halvergate parish. There was a drainage mill, known as Six Mile House Mill, and a marsh man's dwelling, Six Mile House, in this detached parish.

The map below shows the location of the Cantley Detached Parish.

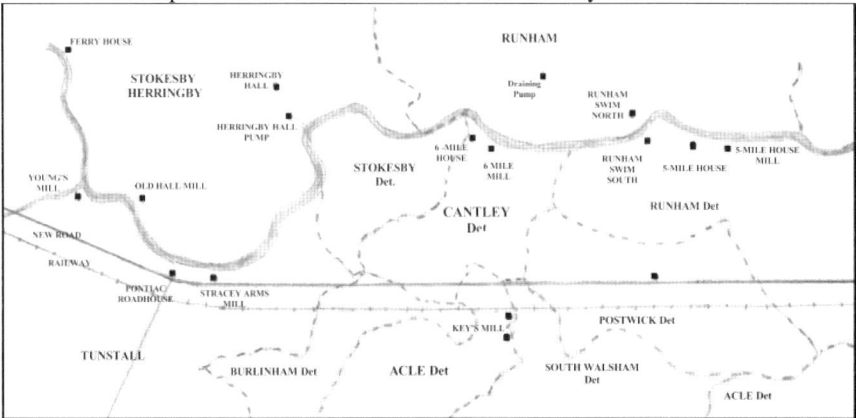

SIX MILE HOUSE DRAINAGE MILL located at TG461098 is shown on the 1996 OS map on the south side of the River Bure. It is a grade 2 listed building.

A mill was marked here on all maps from 1797, and was marked as a 'Drain W Mill' on Faden's 1797 map; as **'CANTLEY MILL'** on Bryant's 1826 map, and as a 'draining pump' in 1884. It has been called by several other names including **BLAKE'S MILL** and **LAKE'S MILL** and **WLLIAM PERRY'S MILL**. On the Cantley Tithe Map & Apportionment, circa 1840, area 233 is marked as 'Mill, House & Yards etc', owned by Mrs Shuckford and occupied by Isaac Gown jnr.

The present mill, believed to have been built in the 1870s, is a tarred redbrick tower mill, four storeys high with an external scoop-wheel. The tower has a lean and corrugated sheeting is on the top. This mill last worked in the mid 1940s. There is now a pump house nearby.

The building firm of R.G. Carter owned the mill, house and several acres here at one time and they sold it in about 1976. The mill is now privately owned.

Smith in 1987 said the mill had no cap, but had stocks and 2 patent sails and internal machinery.

Some of the marshmen here from the Cantley census returns that would have lived in the nearby Six Mile House include: 1851 and 1861 Isaac Gowen; 1871, 1881 and 1891: George Thaxter; 1901 Frederick Bailey.
1911 James David Hewitt.
Mr Robert Lake was the marshman in the 1930s and 1940s..

Six-Mile Mill in Cantley Detached in working order from Brian Grint.

SIX MILE HOUSE TG459099

This lies to the south of the River Bure in the old Cantley detached parish and was marked on the 1797 map, Bryants Map and the 1st OS map of the 1830s. On the tithe Map and Apportionment of circa 1840 the owner was given as Mrs Shuckford and the occupier as Isaac Gown jnr.

The conveyance of freehold hereditaments provides the following early information about the property: In August 1848 conveyance of property from John & Clement Palmer to Isaac Gowen. In 1869 Isaac Gowen leased the property to Geoerge Thaxter for 15 years. In July 1875 the executors of Isaac Gowen auctioned the property and it was purchased by William Parry of Hemsby for £2560.

The house is now owned by Mr Philip Lennard.

David Childs remembers that there was a wide crack in the east wall which was about 6 inch wide at the top. The gable end was shored up in the 1970s.

The house stands on a slightly raised mound. The west gable appears to 18th century but the south face is believed to be of early 19th century, and the north extension of late 19th century build. Excavations in recent years for installing cables and sewers have revealed sherds of grey pottery and layers of black soot believed to predate 1300. Other finds included straw-impressed clamp fired bricks, and burnt red earth with layers of charcoal. It is believed that the finds may point to an early salt boiling site here and perhaps a later brick making site.

Philip Lennard by the excavations at 6-Mile House which are believed to be part of the remains of a salt works here. Peter Allard Collection.

LIMPENHOE

LIMPENHOE VILLAGE SIGN

This recently erected sign is located next to village hall and the children's play area. The village sign shown above depicts the four seasons: Spring has the derelict Limpenhoe drainage mill, Summer shows the Limpenhoe Church, Autumn the village hall, and Winter depicts the marshes. On the top is a Falcon to represent the old Falcon public house and at the bottom is a cluster of fruit to represent community spirit.

The sign board is metal and cast to give an embossed appearance. It was made by Thurton Founderies and designed by Susan McNeil. It is mounted on an oak post, and the base was provided by Cantley Sugar Factory. The project to produce the sign cost about £3,500 paid for by the Cantley Parish Council along with a donation from Pat Bennett. It was unveiled in 2012 by Norfolk newspaper reporter Angela Kennedy.

FARMERS at LIMPENHOE
The following were listed as farmers in census returns and directories.

Name	Dates Listed	Notes
Thomas Rushmer	1832 - 1845	
Francis Drake	1826 - 1861	Low Farm, 295 acres in 1845. Age 71 in 1861, 104 acres.
Benjamin Browning	1832 - 1836	High House Farm
James Neave	1836 - 1849	Hill House Farm, 240 acres in 1845.
Henry Browning	1845	Copyhold house & land.
Daniel Collins	1854	
Richard Cullum	1854	
Isaac Everitt	1849 - 1861	Age 59, 300 acres in 1861 at Hill House.
Daniel Playford	1854 -1865	Age 45, 46 acres in 1861.
Robert Waters	1865 - 1883	Age 70 in 1871, 65 acres. At Low Farm, age 80 in 1881.
Benjamin Ayden	1861 - 1865	Age 53 in 1861, 8 acres.
Henry Fisk	1861 - 1865	Age 47, 56 acres in 1861.
Dick Bullard Esq.	1864 - 1869	Hill House.
William Scarle	1869	
William George Wiseman	1871 - 1877	Age 22, 300 acres. Hill House.
William Henry Harrison	1869 - 1881	Age 28, 59acres
Henry Waters	1877	
Charles Ward	1877	
William Carter	1883 - 1888	Church Farm.
Thomas Peart	1881 - 1883	Age 52 in 1881, 70 acres.
Sophia Bullard	1881 - 1891	Age 45 in 1881, Hill Farm, 480 acres, employs 15 men & 7 boys.
William Curtis	1881	Age 42 in 1881, 20 acres.
David Tills	1888 - 1896	Age 61 in 1891, Low Farm.
Albert Shearing	1891 - 1916	Age 25 in 1891, Marsh Farm.
Elizabeth Carter	1888 - 1937	Age 47 in 1891, Church Farm.
James Brown	1891	Age 58 in 1891.
Last Mallett	1891 - 1896	Age 39 in 1891.
Samuel Sexton	1891	Age 50 in 1891
William Fowler	1891	Age 74 in 1891.
Robert Forder	1896 – 1900	
Arthur William May	1896 - 1916	Hill House Farm.
Henry Hall	1900	
Cornelius Sutton	1900	Low Farm
John Youngs	1900	

Anna Elizabeth Monsley	1912 - 1915	Low Farm.
Samuel Falgate	1912	
Joseph Bates	1916	Church Farm. Bailiff H.S. Tills.
Robert Wilkin Haylett	1929	Willows Farm.
Robert Lambert Wymer	1929 - 1937	Low Farm.
Henry Bates	1929	Cantley View Farm.
Charles William May	1929 - 1937	Hill House Farm.
Ruben Edwards	1937	Cantley View Farm, bailiff.
B. J. Key	Currently.	Wood Farm on Cantley Road.
Mr Dunthorne	Currently	Hill House Farm

MARSH FARM at TG395035

On the 1845 Tithe map this area where the house is now located was marked as Allotments, and the adjacent area, 51, was listed as a cottage and garden. The cottage was owned and occupied at that time by William Jermyn. The farmhouse appears on the 1880s OS maps and all subsequent OS maps but the name Marsh Farm first appears on the 1970s Map.

The owner of the farm in 1912 and 1915 was a Mr John Walker of Norwich, and the occupier was Albert Shearing.

In 1996 the farmhouse was put up for sale as a two bedroom freehold property for £90,000.

Marsh Farm. Supplied by Joy Brock.

HILL HOUSE FARM at TG402030

This was shown on area 80 of the 1845 Tithe map, owned by J. F. Leathes of Reedham and occupied by James Neave.

It was for sale in 1848 as lot5 when the Reedham Hall Estate was auctioned. (NRO/STA703)

It was called at that time "**The Hill House Farm**" and described as a *Farm residence of brick and slate, recently renovated containing: Entrance Hall, Two Parlours, Storeroom, spacious Kitchen, Wash-house with pump therein, Dairy, Four Bedrooms, four Attics, a paved yard with pump of water, excellent Garden with Toolhouse etc. A new riding Stable, two loose boxes, Hay house, Harness-house, Gig House, granary, two good barns, piggeries, Fowl House, enclosed yards, Turnip-house, Bullock Sheds, Waggon Lodge, Three brick & slate lean-to stables, two cart-horse stables, harness-house, Chaff bin and Carpenters shop.*

The property included 283a 2r 18p of land in Limpenhoe and Reedham and was in the occupation of James Neeve.

In 1849 Hill House was conveyed to Isaac Everitt (NRO/STA692).

The owner of the farm was listed as the Rev. William Charles Emeris in 1912 and 1915.

The farm, much altered over the years, is now in the occupation of Mr Dunthorne,

CHURCH FARM

No buildings were shown here on the Tithe Map. The farm house and buildings, located at about TG397039, appear on the 1880s OS map and all subsequent maps. The first known occupants were the Carter family, and the widowed Mrs Elizabeth Carter remained here for many years. According to the 1916 directory, although Mrs Carter still resided at the Farm house, a Mr Joseph Bates farmed Church Farm and Herbert Salmon Tills was at that time his bailiff.

Recent occupants of the farm house are Mr & Mrs R. J. Howard then Mr & Mrs Garner. The house was sold in 1998 for £110,000 and again in 2006 for £375,000.

Mrs Elizabeth Carter. From Joy Brock.

Church Farm House in 2006.

LOW FARM at TG398036

On the tithe map a cottage was marked on area 62 which is where the farmhouse is located. This was owned by the Maddison family and occupied by Francis Drake.

In 1915 the farm house was occupied by Anna Elizabeth Monsey.

The Farmhouse was sold in 2002 as a 4 bedroom freehold property for £308,000 and it is now a 5 bedroom house valued at £595,000.

Low Farm in 2001.

CANTLEY VIEW FARM

This is located to the west of the old rectory. No farmhouse was shown on the Tithe Map of circa 1845 at this location, area 44. At that time this area was owned by John Francis Leathes and farmed by Francis Drake and only had a 'cart-shed' located there. The farm first appears with this name on the 1970s OS map.
In recent years some of the farmland, owned by Mr N. P. Key, has been converted into a fishing lake and holiday lodges built.

JOY BROCK REMEMBERS

We moved from Limpenhoe to Freethorpe in 1946, but because of relatives and friends living there I still remember Limpenhoe well, and with affection.

I can just remember my great grandmother Carter. My great grandparents, William and Elizabeth Carter moved from Limpenhoe Hill to Church Farm House in 1882. Just over 5 years later my great grandfather caught a chill and had pleurisy and died age 49 years. His widow stayed at Church Farm until she died fifty years later aged 95. During that time she had various members of the family there as she was not happy without a man living in the house. Albert and Mary-Ann, her eldest daughter, Shearing went to live with her after they left Marsh Farm next to Limpenhoe Staithe (probably in the early 1920s). Then in the 1930s her daughter, Ada, and her husband Frank Cater moved from their shop in Freethorpe to Church Farm House as well.

My grandmother, who was the youngest of five, was only nine when her father died. Her oldest brother, also called William Carter, had a shop on the Common before moving to a farm at Moulton, and her brother Henry married and moved into the shop which later also became the Post Office. Before then her sister Mary-Ann had married Albert Shearing and moved into Limpenhoe Marsh Farm near the river. They took in visitors in the summer, as well as keeping cows and selling coal. This farm house,

**Charles Brock circa 1930.
Supplied by Joy Brock.**

which was on the footpath through to Cantley factory, is no longer there. When I was living in Limpenhoe there was somebody by the name of Fox living there. My grandmother's sister Jane left Limpenhoe when she married Tom Sutton, who was a butcher in Loddon.

JOY BROCK and ANN RUSSELL (nee BROCK) REMEMBER

Our grandparents, Charles and Anna Brock (nee Carter), married in 1903 and moved into Marsh Farm (not the Marsh Farm by the river), which consisted of their small home and three marshes, and just kept cows, sold milk and made butter, which was sold at Anna's brother's shop on the Common. The shop was not yet the Post Office at this stage. Granddad carried on working as a tailor having learnt from his father in Freethorpe. A few weeks after they married, Nanna Brock's brother William went missing. He had gone on the train to Yarmouth and as it was very foggy it was assumed that he had walked into the river. His body wasn't found until several weeks later.

Our father, Alec was born at Marsh Farm in 1904, followed by his sisters Eva and Jessie. Both Eva and Jessie married from Marsh Farm. When our father married Ivy Youngs from Halvergate Post office they moved into Red House in Limpenhoe, which had been built for Mrs Ann Monsey (previously of Low Farm) in 1912. Our parents were Methodists and teetotallers and so they changed the name of the house to Hillcrest because the Red House was the name of public house in Cantley. We were both born at Hillcrest. This property is now called Chapelfield House.

Dad worked in the office at Cantley Factory and met Nat Bircham, skipper of the wherry Albion, which was used to bring sugar beet to the factory. In dad's spare time he was an insurance agent and for several years insured the Albion with Norwich Union.

Limpenhoe School, which Dad and Nanna attended, had recently closed when Joy started school in 1936, so she went on a school bus to Freethorpe. Mum, like other mothers in those days, did not go out to work.

The Red House circa 1930.

About the same time as Dad was changing his job and moving to Freethorpe our grandparents wanted to retire. As they had not been able to sell Marsh Farm they swapped with Albert and Rosalie Mallett who lived in a thatched bungalow. They had not lived there long, when one Sunday afternoon in February 1949 they, as usual, had gone to the Methodist chapel, and Miss Nora Gotts, a school teacher from Cantley, who was the organist that day, came home with them for tea. They had an open fire and a spark from it must have set the thatch alight, unknown to them. It was a cold windy day and granddad is reputed to have said "It is beginning to get warm at last", when someone knocked on their door to say their roof was on fire. The whole bungalow burnt down very quickly and some of the things they managed to get out of the bungalow were still burnt when the burning thatched roof slid onto them.

As it was school half-term, Joy was free to go with Nanna and look at what was left the next morning. Where the pantry would have been, they found a cocoa tin containing a half-sovereign and three half-crowns. When she had been able to go on the train to Norwich she always had one and a half sovereigns in her handbag. Unfortunately she had sold the sovereign for £1 – 7s – 6d and this had been put in the cocoa tin, but the pound note had been burnt.

Albert and Mary Ann Shearing in later years. From Joy Brock,

A brick and tile bungalow was quickly built by granddad's brother and nephew (Jack Brock builders of Freethorpe). Granddad lived there for the rest of his life and Nanna until her late eighties. The bungalow belonged to dad and he let Ann and her husband Bill Russell in as tenants in 1971.

Next Page: Wedding Photograph of Mervyn Cooke and Jessie Brock in May 1940, supplied by Joy Brock.
Back Row from Left: Walter Hewitt, Lennie Shearing, Fred Cooke, unknown, unknown, Robert Cooke, unknown, Joe Addy, Alec Brock, William Farrow, Rev George Jackson, Lily Sutton, Nettie Eagle (nee Carter), Dolly Hubbard (nee Newson).
Middle Row: Beryl Shearing, Arthur Brock, Libby Brock, Ivy Brock, Winnie Gowing, Rose Brown, unknown, Evelyn Sargent (nee Cooke), Jane Sutton, Charlie Brock, berli Manthorpe (nee Sutton), Eva Farrow (nee Brock), Mary Ann Shearing, Basil Hubbard, Ada Carter (nee Shearing), Frank Carter.
Next Row: Mrs Walter Hewitt with baby Reggie, Betty Carter, Ocie Cooke, Peggy Farrow, Mervyn Cooke, Jessie Brock, Joy Brock, Annie Brock, June Eagle, Alice Clarke, Bella Brock.
Front Row: Peter Farrow, Mavis Hubbard, Dawn Manthorpe.

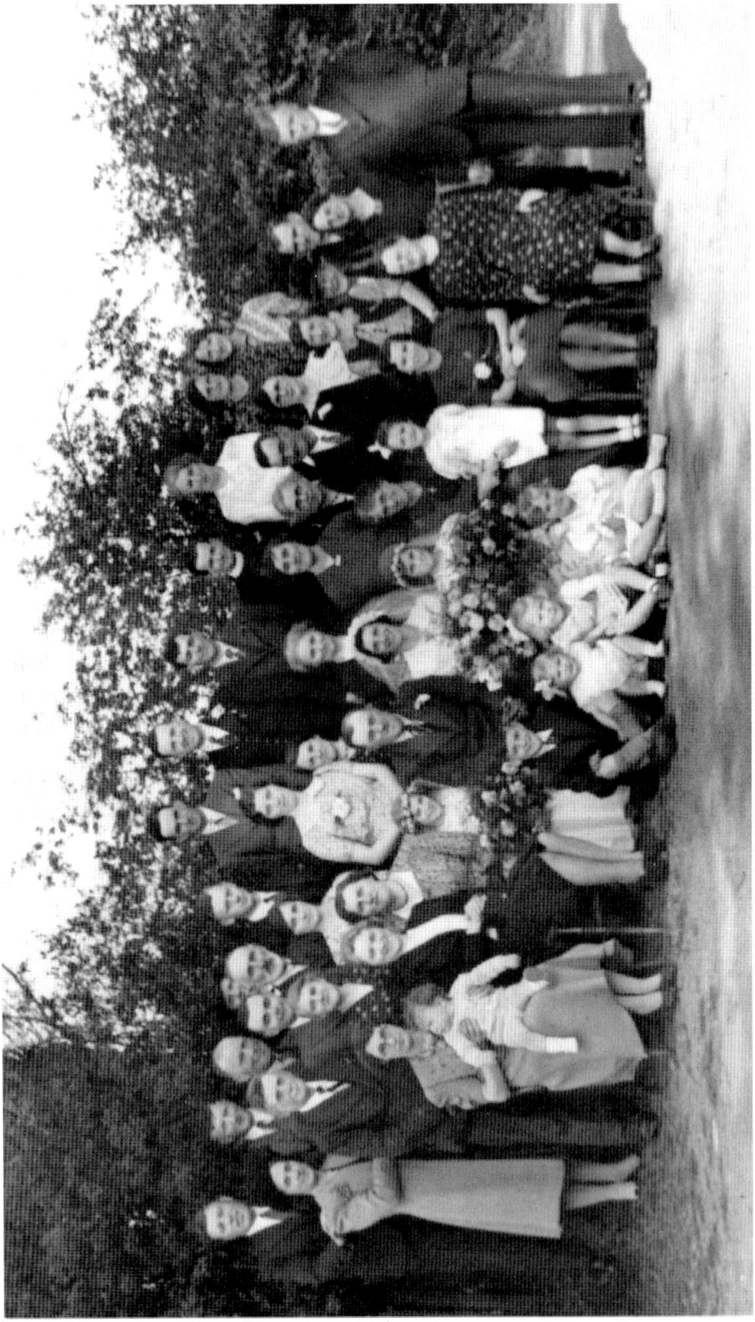

ST BOTOLPH CHURCH, LIMPENHOE

This Grade II listed building is located at about TG395040. The church is flint with stone dressings consisting of chancel, nave, porch and tower. The lower part of the tower is believed to be of 15th century origin. The church was rebuilt around 1881, the architect being Arthur South Hewitt of Norwich.

The church was not drawn on the Tithe Map of circa 1845, but stood on area 59, which was marked as Glebe and owned by the Rev John Johnson and occupied by Francis Drake; and the 1845 directory does not describe the church. The church did exist then, however, and was marked here on the 1848 map, which was produced when the Reedham Hall Estate was put up for sale. Ref. NRO STA703. It is probable that the church was in a neglected state and the population probably used Southwood church during this period. It was re-pewed in 1851 by subscription. The 1854 directory reports: *'The church, dedicated to St Botolph, is a discharged vicarage, valued in the king's book at £6 13s. 4d., and annexed to Southwood rectory. Here are twelve acres of glebe let in small allotments to the poor'*

On 19th July of 1852, during some repair work, three wall mural paintings were found on the north wall of the old church and were reported by the Very Rev Frederick Charles Husenbeth and published in Norfolk Archaeology in 1859. The 3 paintings were said to represent the martyrdom of St Catherine. One of the sketches, of the first mural between the north door and window is shown below. Some areas were not visible and the three 'floating' heads in this mural were reported to be from a later painting. Illegible black lettering was also revealed.

Mural Paintings, North Wall, Limpenhoe Church, Norfolk.

The 1865 directory reports that: *'The church is a small building consisting only of a nave and a small ivy-covered tower. The register dates from 1657. The living is a discharged vicarage annexed to the rectory of Southwood'*.

This 'ivy covered tower' description is again indicative that the church was being neglected.

The Churches of Norfolk Vol. II published in 1911 gives the following brief description: *'The old church, which was a most interesting little thatched building showing on the South side a good Norman doorway and three windows belonging respectively to the 13th, 14th, and 15th centuries, with the lower part of a very fine 15th century tower was most unfortunately cleared away for a successor in 1881. The Norman doorway was re-erected, but in a much restored condition.* '

Sketch of the original thatched Limpenhoe Church before restoration.

When the old thatched roof was removed during renovations the walls collapsed and very little of the original building remained standing, so the present church was effectively a rebuild. The church has two bells, one of which came from Southwood Church. The stained glass window was given in 1898 by Rev. Day in memory of his parents, and the pulpit was re-carved in that same year. The organ was also a gift from the Rev. Theodore Day.

The burial ground was increased in 1911and again in 1946
The benefice of Cantley and the Limpenhoe and Southwood benefice were united in 1934, and in 1981 the benefice of Reedham was incorporated. In the year 2002 the united benefice of Cantley, Freethorpe, Halvergate, Tunstall, Southwood, Limpenhoe, Reedham and Wickhampton was formed.

Limpenhoe Church before the burial ground was increased in 1946.

Some Limpenhoe clergymen	Date
Henry de Bynham	1311
Jeffrey de Carleton	1311
John Bernard	1326
Ralph Ive	1342
Henry de Ormesby	1349
Richard Cook	1378
John Everard	1379
John Messager	1385
William Gladchere	1388
Simon Pessey	1393
William Haverpenny	1396
William Tiffeyn	1398
Laurence Skot.	1402
Elyas Mason	1410
John Claypole	1417
John Cade	1419
William Dolyner	1426
Thomas Skarnynge	1432
William Spink	1441
John Maynhowse/ Crostwayte	
Christopher Browne	1550
John Cooke	
John Cullimer (or Cullyner)	1600
Henry Goodere	1630
William Keen	1636

Thomas Rayner	1657
Edward Walters	1670
James Dover	1693
Thomas Morden	1735
Edward Leathes	1779
James Reading	1788
William Farley Wilkinson	1790
John Love	1803
George Reading Leathes	1803
John Munnings Johnson	1836
Rupert James Rowton	1847
Francis Smith	1854
Charles Abraham Brook	1853
Carteret Henry Leathes	1856
Theodore Henry Crossman Day	1871
Charles V. Parkerson Day	1906
Fennell Fitzpatrick	1907
Thomas Housecraft	1910
Edward Powell	1931
Edwin John Gargery	1934
Huburt Woodall Bevan	1945
Lewis Llewellyn Thomas	1951
Howard W. Sanderson	1955
Colin Francis Scott	1959
Ernest G. Linden Ball	1962

LIMPENHOE POOR' LAND

In the parliamentary returns of 1786 there is mention of some land being given to the poor of the parish, then vested in Elizabeth Maddisson and producing 5s. per year. There was half an acre of land belonging to Francis Drake, and formally the property of the Maddisson family for which Francis Drake pays 10s. per annum rent, and the rent monies received is paid out in threepenny loaves and distributed in the month of April, amongst the poor of the parish who are selected by the churchwarden, Mr Drake.

LIMPENHOE WAR MEMORIAL

This is located in the churchyard and has the following names from the 1914-18 Great War:
Walter Herbert Webb, John William Spooner, Hylton Hayward May, Frederick W.N. Barker, William Eric Postle, and John Daniel Loades.

LIMPENHOE RECTORY

The rectory was not identified on the Tithe Map of circa 1845. A building was, however, marked on Area 58, which is where the rectory is located, and this was stated as 'House, Yard & Barns' and owned by the John Francis Leathes and occupied by the farmer Francis Drake.

The buildings shown on the Tithe map were known, in 1848 when the Reedham Hall Estate was put up for sale, as '**THE CHURCH FARM**'. (NRO/STA703)

The building was part of Lot 3 in the sale and was described as follows; *'The Church Farm comprises an excellent brick and slate residence containing Entrance Hall, two parlours, storerooms, kitchen, wash-house with pumps of water, dairy, beer and wine cellars, 7 bedrooms, dressing room, cheese room, two closets and domestic offices'* There was also a garden and numerous outbuildings associated with the house.

Lot 3 also included a total of 308 acres of land in Limpenhoe, Reedham and Southwood along with a cottage at Oxpits. The occupant at the time of the auction was the farmer and churchwarden Mr Francis Drake.

The 1864 directory reports that 'the Rectory House is situated in this parish and is a good residence, which was purchased and altered in 1852, at a cost of £1000'.

The house is believed to have been part rebuilt, extended and significantly altered. An examination of the 1845 tithe map and the 1880s OS map show the building has a very different footprint on the two maps indicating that major alterations had taken place.

One part of the existing building is believed to be of eighteenth century build and the larger part is Victorian. It is redbrick with a tiled roof.

When Limpenhoe was consolidated with Southwood an extra wing was added, but this wing was later demolished in the 1950s. A comparison of the 1951 and 1972 OS maps again shows the footprint of the building has changed.

When the Cantley Benefice was united with the Limpenhoe and Southwood Benefice in 1934, the Limpenhoe rectory became the parsonage for the united benefice, and the Cantley parsonage was eventually put up for sale.

The Old Rectory at Limpenhoe was sold in 1976 as a private dwelling. In 2008 it was sold for a price of £616,750, and again in 2012 as a 5 bedroom house, it was for sale for a price of £500,000.

A '**Reading Room**' was marked on the 1907 OS map, and later maps through till the 1960s, located immediately to the west of the rectory and where Cantley View farm is now marked. This was referred to in the 1904 and 1929 directories as the '**Parish Room**, an iron building affording 80 sittings'.

Limpenhoe Rectory in 2007. The left side is Georgian and the right is Victorian.

LIMPENHOE PRIMITIVE METHODIST CHAPEL

A Primitive Methodist chapel has existed in the village for many years, as the 1836 directory, and all subsequent directories, each mention a "small chapel" in the village. There have been 2 chapels in the village over the years. The first was on Limpenhoe Common in what is now the garden of Magnolia Cottage on Well Road.

The derelict Limpenhoe Methodist Chapel in 2011.

A new chapel was built at about TG399036 on the Reedham Road, the road between the Common and Limpenhoe Hill. This was built on area 75 of the Limpenhoe Tithe Map, owned by John Francis Leathes and occupied by the farmer Francis Drake. This second chapel was built of Suffolk white bricks and had two rooms, one large for meetings, and one small. It also had a detached privy. It was opened in 1877 and continued in use until about 1994. The last service was held here on September 11th 1994.

In 1986 electricity was installed by D. J. Pritchard.

In December 1996 it was advertised for sale for £70,000. The property was eventually purchased by Mr Dunthorne of Limpenhoe Hill Farm and converted into a dwelling.

The Sunday School Anniversaries were held in the barn at Limpenhoe Church Farm because the small chapel was not big enough to have held the congregation.

Inside Limpenhoe Primitive Methodist Chapel. From Joy Brock.

Limpenhoe Primitive Methodist Chapel in 1989.

Sunday School Anniversary 14th July 1965 at Church Farm Barn Limpenhoe. Mr Sloper is the leader. Photograph supplied by Joy Brock.

Outside Church Farm Barn during a Methodist Chapel Anniversary. Supplied by Joy Brock.

LIMPENHOE SCHOOL AND VILLAGE HALL

The **Limpenhoe** National School, located at about TG395035, was built in red brick around 1850, and reported in the 1864 directory to have cost £150, and had only two rooms. It was built on area 57 of the tithe map which was owned by John Francis Leathes, the Lord of the Manor. It served both Limpenhoe and Southwood. In 1864 it was attended by about 40 pupils.

In 1894 it was enlarged to accommodate 60 pupils. In 1903 it still had only two classrooms and was reported to accommodate up to 62 pupils. A school house was built at Limpenhoe in 1899 for the school headmistress. This is believed to have been to the west of the rectory and adjacent to the Reading Room, and which is now the location of Cantley View Farm.

The school was used until 1931 when local children went to Freethorpe School. The school had a head teacher, an assistant teacher and a monitor, which was usually one of the older girl pupils. The school had a manager, who was Mr Albert Shearing during the 1920s, and the rector made regular visits. A log book was kept to record the general activities and this was kept by for many years J. P. Housecroft. (NRO/MF1474/8)

The old school building later became the village hall. In 1955 the local residents raised £200 to purchase the building for the village and in 1960 a charitable trust was set up to look after the property and make it the Village Hall. In 2001 the village hall was extended and refurbished with the aid of a Lottery grant of £156,000, and another £10,000 raised by the local residents.

Some Limpenhoe School Teachers.

Name	Dates listed	Notes
Henry Alden	1854	School master
Elizabeth Barnes	1861- 1865	Age 20 in 1861, schoolmistress
Ruth Barnes	1861	Age 15, schoolmistress
Eliza Fisher	1869	
Harriet Blyth	1871	Age 27, schoolmistress.
Miss Ecclestone	1877	
Mrs Elizabeth Boswell	1883	
Miss Harriet Boswell	1891	Age 25, schoolmistress, boarder at Low Farm with Tills family.
Mabel Jermyn	1890s	Assistant teacher.
Mrs Hannah Tills	1896 – 1920s	Head mistress.
May Moxley	1920s	Assistant teacher.
Miss Doris Humphrey	1920s	Assistant teacher.

Hannah Tills, nee Lumsden, was the headmistress at the school for many years. She was the wife of Herbert Salmon Tills who was once listed as a farm bailiff and later a builder and painter and decorator.

Mrs Tills bought a plot of land in March 1924 from Rev William Charles Emeris and in November 1924 she borrowed £250 from Edmund Reeve, a solicitor of Norwich, in order to build a bungalow on the plot on Freethorpe Road. This bungalow is called The Homestead. In April 1958 the daughter of Hannah Tills, Agnes La Grande Hudson, sold the bungalow for £1,400 to Jack and Monica Gladys Wymer, and in September 2010 Mr and Mrs Tarrant bought the bungalow from the executors of Mr Wymer.

The Homestead on Freethorpe Road.

The school photograph on the following page is believed to date from 1909, and the teacher on the left is the headmistress Hannah Tills.
Photograph supplied by Christine Fisk.

CANTLEY, LIMPENHOE & SOUTHWOOD REMEMBERED

circa 1909

CANTLEY, LIMPENHOE & SOUTHWOOD REMEMBERED

Back Row: Enos Carter, Jimmy Rope, Elsie Sharman, Hellen Mallett, Eva Brown, Stella Spooner, Iris Brister, Ernest Mallett. Gerald Curtis. Next Row: Laura Jermy, May Carter, Iris Mallett,Madeline Gilbert, Doris Brown, Frances Wymer, Gladys Rope, Ivy Jermy, Edna Barker, Margaret Rope.
Next Row: George Curtis, Willie Carter, Jack Wymer, Jack Hudson, Percy Curtis, Vernon Barker, Reggie Jermy.
Front Row: Jimmy Webb, Gordon Mallett, Sidney Webb, Leslie Ellingham, Walter Ellingham, Leslie Webb, John Locke, Walter Carter, Alfred Curtis.

94

JANE RYAN (NEE HOLLIS) CHILDHOOD MEMORIES

I was born 16th March 1946 at Limpenhoe Corner at my grandparents' home. They were Laura Daisy, and Samuel Ellis Jermy, being my mother's mother and father. In their family there were three sons Russell, Reggie and Frank, and three daughters Ivy, Laura and Myrtle. My mother married my father Frederick Hollis at Limpenhoe Church 19th October 1941.

In 1948 my mother and father moved to Reedham and every day mother walked back to Limpenhoe. As soon as I was old enough I spent a lot of time back at Limpenhoe. By this time my grandparents had moved into the servant quarters at Limpenhoe Rectory, the rector then was Rev.

Left: Samuel & Laura Jermy. Right: Fred and Laura Hollis. Supplied by Jane Ryan.

Gargary. It was a great place to be; it had lovely gardens and many nooks and crannies. My sister Norma and I thought it was a secret garden. Also the Church Fetes were held at the rectory. Gran and granddad were involved with the church and in those days there were three services on a Sunday which we went to. The church bell sounded loudly.

Gran also told me she was like the village mid-wife in her time; always ready to help when called at all hours.

Mrs Ames played the church organ, Mrs Hilda Merry and Kate Waters sang in the Church choir. There were also concerts in the old village hall.

As time passed, my father used to help out at weekends on Lambert Wymer's Farm, especially at harvest. I used to go with him; I remember the horse and carts and all the children on corn field. Gertie Wymer used to let me collect the hen's eggs. Mrs Gunn kept the post office and it was like a meeting place.

Laura, Myrtle and Ivy Jermy by the school door. From Jane Ryan

As time went on Gran and Granddad moved to Cantley Road Limpenhoe. I had a good friend at Limpenhoe then: Maureen Key, nee Edwards, we had many adventures together. She lived on the Common, her mum and dad were Lou and Sybil Edwards. I also remember picking strawberries with my mother on Mr Burton's Farm. I thought everyone in Limpenhoe were my aunts and uncles: it was such a great community. I still visit the church and tend my grandparents' grave, my parents' graves, my brother Geoff's and Ivy and Myrtles graves. They are all buried there.
My memories of Limpenhoe will last forever

Laura and Ivy Jermy and others, believed to be standing in the doorway of the mat factory which made mats from rushes. Photograph supplied by Jane Ryan.

THE OLD FALCON, LIMPENHOE.

Located on area 60 of the 1844 Tithe map it is marked as **'Falcon Inn and Yards'**, then owned by Francis Drake and occupied by William Church.
Note: although it was not indicated on either Faden's or Bryant's maps it did exist at those times and was owned by John Day's St. Martins Brewery of Norwich.
On the 2nd October1795 Mr John Day made absolute surrender of the Falcon to Mr John Patteson, and on the 3rd May 1821 Patteson conveyed it to a Samuel Paget. Some time later Francis Drake became the owner.

The Old Falcon before it closed as a pub, from Brian & Pat Bennett.

Francis Drake made a deed of covenant of conditional surrender of The Falcon to Isaac Bugg of Norwich in 1864. Isaac Bugg having changed his name to Isaac Bugg Coakes, in April 1868 conveyed the property to William Sales, who had taken out a mortgage of £300 for the property. On the 14th July 1890 William Sales conveyed the pub to Morgans Brewery.

During the twentieth century it was owned by Morgans Brewery, then Steward & Patteson, and finally by Watney Mann. In 1972 when it ceased to be a public house it was sold by Watney Mann to Mr and Mrs P. M. Stevens as a dwelling.

The current occupants are Mr and Mrs Brian and Pat Bennett who bought the old pub in 1993.

Name Licensee/ Occupant	Dates Listed	Notes
EDWARD TROTT	1789	
ROBERT CLARKE	1790	
	1819	Up for sale.
THOMAS SCARL(E)	1836 - 1841	Age 50 in 1841, FALCON
WILLIAM CHURCH	1845 - 1846	
JOHN HALES	1847 - 1856	Age 38 in 1851,& butcher.
WILLIAM SCARLE	1858 - 1861	Age 48 in 1861 & labourer.
WILLIAM SALES	1864 - 1889	Age 40 in 1871. & blacksmith.

GEORGE PEARCE	11.11.1889	Age 50 in 1891.
WILLIAM HENRY RICKWOOD	13.11.1899	& bootmaker.
WILLIAM WATERS GOOCH	21.01.1901	Age 51 in 1901.
JOHN CHARLES DEEKS	16.03.1903	
THOMAS JOSEPH HUNTING	07.11.1904	
FREDERICK HOWES	12.03.1906	
HERBERT EDWARD FIELD	10.02.1908	Age 26 in 1911.
JAMES LACEY	04.11.1912	
FREDERICK SAMUEL WYMER	11.01.1932	
AUSTIN LEONARD BURGESS	28.09.1959	
GEOFFREY DODDING	24.04.1972	
	1972	Closed.

Austin Leonard Burgess behind the bar. From Brian & Pat Bennett.

Located at the junction of Well Road, Freethorpe Road and Church, the building is constructed of brick and slate and is painted white. The building has changed much

over the years but at the rear of the building there is an old brick barrel fluted cellar still in existence which is half below and half above ground,
It is currently owned by Brian and Pat Bennett and called **Falcon House**. Here they now have two holiday apartment lets built on the grounds; and previously they ran a taxi business from here called Falcon Cars.

Ode by Austin Burgess:
"If you don't know where to go,
Try the Falcon at Limpenhoe,
Just in case you've not been told,
It's a rendez-vous for Young and Old."

ANCHOR OF HOPE, LIMPENHOE

Ii is believed that another public house existed in the parish in the early nineteenth century. This was either called the **Anchor of Hope** or the **Anchor and Hope**. In the 1845 directory **Henry Rushmer** was listed as a beer-seller but no public house of this name appears in any of the old directories or in the early census returns. On the Limpenhoe Tithe map, circa 1844, Henry Rushmer was listed as the owner and occupier of cottages on areas 65 and 65a one on each side of Well Road at the Common so it is possible that one of these cottages may have been the beer-house.
Cherry Tree Cottage, on the east side of Well Road, is on area 65 of the Tithe Map and it is possible that this was the location of Henry Rushmer's beerhouse.
John England in the 1861census, age 62, was listed as living in Limpenhoe at the "**Anchor of Hope**", as a coal merchant but there was no mention of it being a beerhouse in those census returns. This same John England was age 52 in 1851, listed as a publican & Waterman, at the Red House pub in Cantley, and in the 1864 directory he was listed at Limpenhoe as a wherry owner and beerseller so it quite possible that he moved here and took over this as a beer-house.

Albert Eagle & Nettie Carter in the grounds of the post office with Cherry Tree cottage in background

The licence register refers to a beer-house of this name and says that it was closed before 1872, and converted into a private dwelling.

LIMPENHOE DRAINAGE MILL (EAST).

This is located at about TG397019
A drain mill was marked here at this location on the 1797 map. A mill was also marked here on the 1825 map with the name marked alongside, presumably the occupier, James Neave, and the land was owned by John Francis Leathes.
It was not marked, however, on the Bryant's 1826 map!

In NRO/STA731, dated 22 Sept 1842, 'Mill House Farm' was given as 306A 3R 3P and the rent was £305. The owner was John Francis Leathes, the Lord of the Manor of Reedham and the farm occupier was James Neave.
On the 1844 Tithe Map area 144 was labelled as 'Mill Yard', owned by Leathes and occupied by James Neave. The mill itself was not listed suggesting it had already become obsolete.
When the Reedham Hall Estate was put up for sale by the executors of John Francis Leathes in August 1848 the 'Old Mill Yard' on plot 282 was part of Lot 6 and occupied by James Neave. (NRO/STA703)
The old drainage mill here must have been made obsolete some time after 1825 and demolished.
A 'draining pump', however, was marked here on the 1880s and 1950 OS maps. This was a **steam engine drainage pump** erected some time between 1848 and 1880.

LIMPENHOE DRAINAGE MILL (WEST).

Located at about TG39460190. this is shown on all OS maps, and on the Tithe map.
On the Tithe map, of circa 1845, area 140, was called 'Mill & Yard', and area 138a, was labelled as 'Cottage': both were occupied by William Swash and owned by J. F. Leathes. William Swash was listed in the 1841 census as age 40 a marshman.
The mill was not shown on the earlier Bryant's 1826 and Faden's 1797 maps.
The 4 storey tower is about 35 feet to the curb and had an inside diameter of 16 ft at the base with 22 in thick walls. The tower had three internal floors, the top floor having two windows. The mill had a boat shaped cap and an 8 bladed fantail without a gallery. The four double shuttered patent sails were probably about 10 ft wide with 9 bays of shutters. The drive was via a 19 ft diameter wooden brake wheel to a 5 ft diameter cast iron wallower set on a wooden upright shaft to a second iron wallower driving a 10 ft diameter cast iron pitwheel with wooden teeth

and then to a 19 ft diameter scoopwheel on the same axle. The scoopwheel axle bore the legend *W. ENGLAND 1895.*

Limpenhoe (West) Mill, in working order, and the mill cottage when the Hewitt family lived here circa 1910. Supplied by Doris Goldie, nee Hewitt.

    This drainage mill was originally built by the millwright William Thorold around 1831. The mill was to be paid for by each person in proportion to the acreage of marsh owned that was to be drained by the mill.
    From an Agreement for the Drainage of a certain level of Marshes lying in Limpenhoe & Southwood in the County of Norfolk we have the following. (NRO/MC165/6/1.):
Robert Walpole to pay to John Leathes £25 for 1 acre of marshland, part of areas 138 and 140 on the attached map, to permit the building of a drainage mill and cottage. *'That the specification of William Thorold of the City of Norwich, Engineer hereunto annexed for the erection of a Drainage Mill & Cottage & for making the Drains & Road & other necessary works to be done for the purpose of the said drainage & his contract to perform the same for the sum of £744 is hereby accepted & agreed to by the said parties & that he shall forthwith commence the said works.'*

A person (marshman) had to be appointed by a meeting of the parties to manage the mill and the drains.

The mill, in 1843, is reported to have drained 509a 1r 10p of Limpenhoe and Southwood marshes. (NRO/BR90/47/19)

In 1989, Arthur Smith reported that the cap base frame remained on top of the mill and the iron windshaft was still in place but without its canister, however the brake wheel had collapsed. The floor beams and all the other machinery were still in situ. The 10 in square wooden upright shaft was in two sections and had chamfered corners. A 10 ft diameter pit wheel with a 8½ in square iron shaft connected to an outside 19 ft diameter scoop wheel over an outer iron hoop, with

James Arthur Hewitt at the Limpenhoe Mill. Photograph supplied by Doris Goldie.

many of the wooden paddles still in situ.

Some marsh men listed at the Limpenhoe mill house include:
1901 and 1915: James Arthur Hewitt.
1922: Walter Newson at 'The Mill'.
1929 and 1937: Ernest Charles Mallett.

CANTLEY, LIMPENHOE & SOUTHWOOD REMEMBERED

Hewitt family members by the Limpenhoe Mill scoopwheel clearing out the culvert. Photograph supplied by Doris Goldie.

Limpenhoe Mill on the 27th September 1995. From Peter Allard.

LIMPENHOE DRAINAGE PUMP.

A third drainage pump was located here in Limpenhoe adjacent to the boundary with Cantley parish at about TG391035. This was marked on the 1880s OS map but not on the Tithe map. This pump was built on area 47 of the Tithe map which was owned by John Francis Leathes.

LIMPENHOE STAITHE

This was located at about TG388031 and a farmhouse was nearby. In the 1881 census this house was occupied by farmer Thomas Peart. The Peart family also offered food and accommodation at the farmhouse for the boating community.

LIMPENHOE SHOPS

The former General Stores and Post Office in Limpenhoe, believed to have been built around the 1820's. The Carter Family resided there for many years and by 1914 it had become a Post Office. In later years it reverted back to being a shop and named The Old Post Office. In 1964 it was renamed The White House and was used for residential purposes only. In 1971 The Crossley Family moved in and have been there to the present day. From Jane Crossley.

LIMPENHOE SHOPKEEPERS
The following are found in old directories and census returns.

Name	Date listed	Notes
John Clark(e)	1836 - 1845	
Peter Mallett	1836	Occupied cottages on areas 66 & 67 of tithe map on east side of Well Rd.
Robert Gray	1864 - 1871	Age 43 in 1871, & butcher
George Dingle	1864 - 1865	
Ann Dingle	1869 - 1871	Age 73 in 1871, widow.
Isaac Hanton	1871	Age 30
William Ayden (Hayden)	1871 - 1877	Age 35 in 1871
William Crisp	1877	
John Mallett	1877 -1883	
John Smith	1883	
William Robert Carter	1891 - 1896	Age 30 in 1891, & draper on Common.
Henry Carter	1904 - 1937	& draper; & later the Post Office.
Mrs Eagle	1940s	& Post Office.
Mr & Mrs Gunn	1940s	They lived at Cherry Tree Cottage
Mrs Nicholls	1960s	& Post Office.

Mrs Gunn in 1965. From Bob Waters.

POST OFFICES

The first Limpenhoe Post Office was located at the shop on the west side of Well Road on the Limpenhoe Common and served as a post office from around 1914. This shop was located at area 56 on the tithe map, which was listed at that time as a cottage owned by Ann Wright and occupied by Samuel Mallett. There was a well and pump by the shop which served the community around the Common, and hence the name Well Road.

The post office later moved to the east side of Well Road on

Limpenhoe Common sometime in the 1960s. This property was located at areas 66 and 67 of the tithe map, which at that time were listed as cottages occupied by Peter Mallett.

DAWN TOVELL REMEMBERS

In my childhood years the population of Limpenhoe was about 120. There was one public house, The Falcon, one small shop owned by Mr and Mrs Gunn, where you could get penny packets of crisps and a bottle of Corona for 3d. The Post Office was owned by Mr and Mrs Carter and later by their daughter Mrs Eagle. There was the Anglican Church and the Methodist Chapel.

My earliest recollection is of the War years. My dad was in the Army serving in Europe. One night during the bombing our neighbour, Mr Cunham, came round and carried me round to his house and put me under the table with his two daughters. Minutes later a bomb fell on the Hill doing a lot of damage to one house, although no one was hurt. Afterwards I remember when we went back indoors, pictures had fallen off the walls and things were scattered all about.

One bad winter when the roads were blocked my mother, Hilda Merry, and her friend, Kate Waters, went across the fields to Freethorpe to get provisions and the snow was so deep in places they carried Kate's son Robert and me on their backs.

I attended the Freethorpe School, where we were taken by bus, but when we were eleven we had to bike to the school. To get to Yarmouth or Norwich we had to cycle to either Reedham or Cantley Railway Station to catch the train. To go to the doctors we also had to go to Reedham.

My mother taught in the Church Sunday School so I went to Church from an early age. The church had a choir of adults and children and the organist was Mrs Ames from Reedham. She used to cycle over on Friday nights for choir practice and Sundays for services. She taught me to play the piano and when she retired I played the organ in church. The organ had to be hand blown then, and very often whoever was pumping would let it nearly run out of air on purpose.

My mother also used to organise concerts, producing and writing a lot of her own material. She started off when I was a baby with adults, but later changed to children. We were known as the "Limpenhoe Imps", and we used to hold these concerts in the village hall, which, when mother was young, was the village school. Coronation day in 1953 was a special day, in the afternoon we all went up to the vicarage and played games etc. and we had a fancy dress parade. Then in the evening the whole village went up to Nigel Keys barn at Southwood for a Coronation tea provided by the ladies of the village.

In about 1961 my aunt, Queenie Nicholls, had a shed built in her yard and turned it into a small shop, and she became the post mistress for a few years.

Limpenhoe was a lovely small village, but it has grown a bit more now. I lived there until I was 21, when I got married and I have now lived in Halvergate for 54 years.

BOB WATERS REMEMBERS

My earliest memories of this village are from some time in the early 1940s when our front door was blown off its hinges by the explosion of 2 mines dropped by the Germans on parachutes. One demolished some cottages on The Hill, the other left a hole in the road by the Kill Loke, Freethorpe. I was about 3 years old. Apparently there were 2 Home Guard members on Fire Watch in the school but having consumed a crate of Brown Ale from the Falcon Pub they were in no fit state to attend, (Sid Wright and Louis Gunn).

During the 1940`s we all knew each other: Charlie Brock kept cows at Marsh Farm, Lambert Wymer at Low Farm, Frank Cator at Church Farm, The big landowners were the Mayes family who ran The Hill House Farm. The Falcon pub had Fred Wymer as Landlord: he would split a packet of Woodbines for you, also out of hours beer supply at the back door. On The Common opposite the now White House was an old cottage occupied by Frizzy Brown who had a black frying pan which was used for everything, even washing his face. After his death the family of Alice Rushmer took residence and they were so poor that they burnt the inside doors and the stairs to keep warm. Later the local council erected a Nissen Hut and they survived.

A young Bob Waters.

There was a Post Office kept by the Carters, then by the Eagles: a village pump, and later a Phone Box. Daily deliveries of bread, milk, paraffin were common. There was a parson the Rev. Gargary who just about controlled the village, and employed domestic help, except for a group of Methodists, who had a chapel first on the Common then across the fields, now closed. The school was closed and we all went to Freethorpe.

Additional for the 1940`s was of course the celebration for the ending of WW2 summer of 1945. A party was held at the Vicarage and we all ate some grub and they rang the church bells, Even today I remember some very fat lady singing a solo, all us youngsters just laughed so much it sounded like a Roaring Bull.

We all attended Freethorpe School travelling by bike, later on a bus, the headmaster there was Billy (Goat) Rodgers, a cruel man who hated children, and if you were poor, like most of us were, then he sought to put you down.

Electricity came to the village bringing an end to paraffin lamps etc. Also the council started a dustcart service based at Acle. There was very little waste as most things went on the open fire.

Then the "Gravy Boat" came to empty the toilets: a special adapted lorry with a lid at the back, visiting every Friday; the crew George Pain and Harry always ate lunch near Southwood Plantain. Yes the old Shoddy was the only shed without a lock, and we never lost a pail-full at anytime.

Hilda Merry started a concert party in the old school called The Limpenhoe Imps, it was hilarious, yet each year the place was packed out. Sunday was a very special day nothing moved in the village work-wise. It was Church, Chapel or The Falcon Pub. I often went to worship 3 times on a Sunday: Church in the morning and evening, Chapel in the afternoon, best clothes on. Some of the Methodist local preachers were funny in their Norfolk lingo.

My father Henry Leslie Waters died in 1948. I was the only son of a second marriage so this left me missing out on things that others had. My mother received a meagre widow's pension so I had to work for Frank Cator before and after school, taking and collecting the cows from marsh. Jimmy Hunt who had served as a radio operator in a Lancaster Bomber built mum and I a radio, then one day a man know as a relieving officer called and made us sell it to buy food.

It took me quite a time to get over that!

During the 1950s Limpenhoe was just a joy to live in. There was no Council Tax, phone bills, Electricity shilling in the meter. Coal, paraffin and food was all you needed, money just a small amount that's all. There was a roadman Harry Waters, painter and decorator Herbert Tills, Dairy man Bo Mallett, and another shop G R Gunn, also eggs and milk from Lambert Wymers at Low Farm. Many characters

Henry Leslie Waters in 1929 age 62. Supplied by Bob Waters.

lived there George Canham, (Nigger) who treated animals and had Jackdaws that talked, Harry, Joe and Hannah Harboard who were eccentric to say the least, Arthur Patterson (Gookey)- he chewed tobacco from morn till night and would keep spitting everywhere he went; he kept some part chewed in his hat as a back up. One of the local girl, Dawn Merry I think, had a lovely Tom Cat who suddenly went missing, he returned smelly and scruffy having been mating. He was captured and put in a rubber boot head first, just back legs and tail left out, then part of him was removed using a razor blade followed by a good dose of table salt. When he was shaken out he ran straight through a Gooseberry bush. Thaas done him they said, A local gang evolved as many of us were about the same age, meeting most nights near the now established Phone Box lit up in the winter of course, Known as the Limpenhoe Army we just laughed and laughed, just loved to annoy folks and cause trouble, but not serious, they called us Hobbelly Hoys neither men nor boys. Most boys and girls had a nickname here are a few, Arty Wymer, Bug Waters, Dorg Barker, Rat Rushmer, Frog Rushmer, Toad Barker, Barney Risby, a girl they called Slubroot (Kathy) and Harnser (Gillian).

Favourite pranks were, throwing stones onto the Rushmer's Nissen hut just as The Archers came on the radio, Fireworks in the large keyholes that everyone had, Greasing the pump handle with Cart Grease, Throwing a piece of wire in the air so that it shorted out on the non insulated power cables this caused flickering in all the local houses and out would come folks to investigate. Dialling the operator on the phone and being abusive, 15mins later a black Wolseley Police car would arrive from Acle, not a soul in sight! Throwing eggs and mud at the many cyclists going home from Cantley Factory from the Willow trees in Marsh road.

In 1953 the village of course celebrated the Queens ascension to the throne with a dinner evening in Nigel Keys Barn at Southwood Hall: a grand time was had by all.

Then along came Pop music with Skiffle and Rock n' Roll. I learnt to play Guitar, and there was Sid Mallet on drums, Bob Rushmer on Bass (tea chest and broom handle) David Adams on washboard, and Mick Hewitt on guitar: we met Tuesdays in the old school. What a racket! During that time one of the girls in the village worked in Norwich and brought a young man to one of our Imps Concerts. His name was Johnny Garwood and he played Boogie Woogie Piano. Many were offended: the Vicar thought it was dreadful, but I was hooked and taught myself to play his style. It still comes through today when I play keyboard. Sadly village life was changing: jobs in building, boatyards, and the sugar factory were available so farm work was not the only source of employment. Tractors were quickly replacing Horses, and men were beginning to leave the land jobs.

Kate Waters. Photograph from Bob Waters.

We had been used to only 2 cars in the village: Henry Preston and the Vicar, so many games were played on the road. Leslie Barker who lived in Fairview bungalow at the end of Marsh Road bough a Morris 8 car, well this should never be they said where did he get the money?

I moved to Southwood Corner late 1950s. There were other cottages up there then: The Jermy family and Hooky Thompsons, a shepherd at Southwood Hall. Also further down just past the plantain were Sid Wright and Auty South, real characters, then there were some more cottages near the triangular green housing workers Southwood Hall, Bob Beck, Manny Church and others.

National service was coming to an end but some got called up into the forces. Village life had begun to change. Wednesday nights many of us went to Reedham Pictures films shown in the Legion Hall, Saturday nights was Cantley in the tin hall, quite often the power would fail and there would be fizzy drink and stuff thrown over people during that time.

Well, as the 1950`s came to an end the continued change in lifestyle just happened: men leaving the farms to work in factories commuting by train or car, and private cars were becoming part of every home it seemed. Mid to late 1950s Mrs Gunn, who lived on the Common, had a son captured in the Korean war Billy. She also, took in children from London who had been abused: in particular there was a boy called Thomas Allory. He brought a new language to the village; we had never heard anyone swear like him and even today I smile thinking about some of the things he said. He had been beaten by his father and I never saw him cry even when he lost a fight with other boys, However the local lads got him one night and took him down to the railway line, tied him to the track, and when the next train puffed out of Cantley he screamed like a rabbit being stalked by a stoat, at the last moment he was released – he was never anymore trouble!

Maurice Spooner and daughter Jennifer playing cricket on the road in the 1950s. Supplied by Bob Waters.

My neighbour in the 1960`s was Charlie Broom (Roscoe) who could not read or write. His wife read the paper to him. On the front page of the Daily Mirror one day was a picture of some panthers that escaped from a zoo, Charlie said we would be overrun with them in time just like Coypu so he carried a big stick in case some were in Limpenhoe Spong.

Billy Beck the butcher gave him a transistor radio and one day it said The Beatles were in England very tired (the Liverpool band of course). Charlie found 2 dead beetles in his lavatory next day, "How did they know that?" he said!

The 1960s saw the launch of the first nightclub in the area, (HUT 9). There being nothing much to do in the village for the youngsters at that time Austin Burgess at The Falcon Pub allowed the use of the old Skittle Alley for a club so the local lads led by Mick Bedding (Mim) prepared this building, and at first just a few attended. Wednesday nights became popular so much that 2 car park attendants were needed, or lookouts as it happened. It seems certain films were shown there and the place was packed. A raid by Acle police revealed nothing: the lads had inside info and were just playing darts when they arrived, many laugh about it today.

In 1972 I moved to Freethorpe where I still live. Property prices had risen and old farm cottages were selling for lots of money instead of a few hundred pounds and fields were being made bigger by removing hedges and trees, this of course brought in folks who were not country people and village life had changed.

BOB WATERS. February 2014

Sid Mallett. Photo from Bob Waters.

BLACKSMITHS

Limpenhoe, like Cantley had a blacksmith.

On the tithe map, area 71, on the common at the junction of Marsh Road and Well Road was listed as 'blacksmith shop', owned by Bunning Maddison Devises and occupied by Francis Drake. There may have been another blacksmith's shop at the Falcon Inn as William Sales was listed there as both victualler and blacksmith in the 1864 directory.

Some possible blacksmiths in the parish include:

CANTLEY, LIMPENHOE & SOUTHWOOD REMEMBERED

Name	Dates listed	Notes
John Sales	1815	From Parish Register
William Rushmer	1821	"
James Spooner	1829	"
Samuel Tills	1831	"
Daniel Spooner	1815 - 1861	Age 64 in 1861 census.
William Sales	1861 - 1883	Age 43 in 1861, & Coal Merchant at the Old Falcon.

TRANSCRIPT OF AN IMPS PROGRAMME FROM THE 1950S

THE LIMPENHOE "IMPS" VARIETY SHOW

Producer   Hilda Merry
Skiffle Leader   Robert Waters
Pianist   Dawn Merry
PROGRAMME
The Queen
1. Opening Number   The Company
2. Skiffle Interlude   "Bob" & His Boys
3. The Sailor's Hornpipe   Janet, Peggy & Maureen
4. Song – "Only You"   Robert
5. "Me and My Old Dutch"   Maureen & Michael
6. Monologue or Humerous Interlude   Hilda Merry
7 Sketch – "Mary's Sister John"   'The Quins'
****
INTERVAL
8. "The Operation"   Dr. Canham & Co.
9. Song – Tammy (Guitar Accomp)   Dawn
10. "They're Wonderfull" Comody Song)   "The Trio"
11. Short Skiffle Interlude.   "Bob" & His Boys
12. "The Vagabond Trio"   Dawn, Janet & George
13. "The Widow's Mistake"   Hilda Merry, George & Peggy
14. "Oh! What a Life for a Lady"   "The Trio"
15. Song – selected   Kate Waters
16 Finale "Madame Zana's Waxworks"   The Company
15 Minute Skiffle Session.
PROGRAMME   4d.

ELECTRICITY

Electricity came to the villages in the mid 1930s.
Residents had to apply to the Corporation Electricity Office in Norwich if they wanted an electric supply to their property. They were permitted to have up to 4 electric points installed free of charge, and must have two points in the living room; one as alight and one as a socket. The annual rent was 2 shillings per electric point. Extra points could be installed at an extra cost.

MAINS WATER SUPPLY

Mains water came in the early 1960s. Residents had to apply to the council if they wanted a mains supply. Very isolated properties were excluded.
The water company laid the mains along the roadsides to the curtilage, or to within 60 feet of the curtilage of the property free of charge. The pipework to the property and taps etc. had to be provided and funded by the householders themselves.

LIMPENHOE TIME CAPSULE

A time capsule was buried at midday on 21st March 1999 containing contributions from several members of the community, young and old, with the intention of retrieving the contents on 21st March 2050. The following notes were recorded for the time capsule by Christine Fisk during discussions with the two oldest members of the community.

SOME RECOLLECTIONS OF LIFE IN LIMPENHOE.
Jack Wymer, born 17th May 1920 at Low Farm, Limpenhoe and Peter Race who moved to Limpenhoe in 1957.

The late **Jack Wymer** was born at Low Farm, Limpenhoe on 17th May 1920. Here he lived until 1942 when he married Monica, a school teacher, they had one son Michael.
    After Jack and Monica got married they moved to Cantley for two years and rented rooms at the Grange. Then they moved back to Limpenhoe and lived for many years in one of the cottages on The Common (now known as Don's Cottage). Jack moved in 1957 to his current bungalow (which was built in 1935 for Hannah Tills, the Head Mistress of Limpenhoe School) which is at the Reedham end of Freethorpe Road.
    Jack's nickname as a lad was 'Limpo' and from 1925 to 1931 he went to

Limpenhoe School, (which we now know as the village hall). The School was built shortly after 1850 and taught the ages of 5 - 14. There were 25/30 children attending in Jack's day. There were two school rooms and two teachers, one of whom was the Head Mistress Hannah Tills. The basic 3 R's were taught and Religious instruction was carried out by the Rev. Housecroft. Oil lamps were used for lighting and Jack remembers having to wash in a well outside at the back of the school (this was rain water run off). The Head Mistress was Hannah Tills, who is buried in Limpenhoe Churchyard in a grave containing 5 people: her mother Mrs. Lumsden, Hannah, her husband, her son (a Metropolitan Policeman) and his wife. Hannah died from a heart attack while she was travelling to London on a train). In 1931 the school was closed and Jack went to Freethorpe School until 1934. Jack was one of eight children and they all had to lend a hand around the farm. Before and after school Jack had to do his share of the milking. He remembers that they always had enough to eat though - eggs, milk, butter, cheese, chickens, game and a pig hanging in the dairy.

Ploughing the fields in those early days was all done with horses. A 9" one furrow plough, harnessed to two horses with an experienced driver could expect to do an acre per day. Do you know how far they walked? Over ten miles per acre!

The hub of Limpenhoe was 'The Comrnon' - this is now a piece of tarmac outside the White House (where Cyril and Jane Crossley live). In those days the village had a Post Office, two shops, a pub, a Chapel and a Church Hall. The Post Office and shop were originally in Carter's House (the White House front garden now). Henry Carter (known as "Crinks") was a local farmer (and a Limpenhoe Chapel man). His son Wilfied Carter (known as "Chiney") was Station Master at Cantley and then Norwich.

Henry Carter also owned Church Farm and although he farmed the land the house was rented out to Albert Shearing.

The Post Office and shop was then relocated to a shed in the garden of the semi-detached cottages behind "Cherry Tree Cottage" (there was also a red telephone box in the garden until the 1980's.) At this time the Post office and shop were run by Queenie, who moved here from Reedham. The original Chapel was behind Cherry Tree Cottage. Cherry Tree Cottage at that time was rented by George Gunn (owned by Alec Brock) who had a greengrocers round and also sold produce from the cottage. His son Billy Gunn was captured at Dunkirk and was a prisoner of war for 5 years. He was demobbed but remained in the reserves, was called up again to go to Korea, where he was once again taken as a POW.

Lewis Gunn (known as "Porky"), who was Billy's brother, left in the mid 50's and went to live in Gt. Yarmouth.

Prior to Billy Gunn living at Cherry Tree Cottage it was one of the two dairy farms in Limpenhoe (the other being Marsh Farm) and was owned by Ira Moll. The present garden was a bullock yard with buildings all around the edge. Ira used to own the marsh opposite and also use the Carnser for grazing (the marsh is now owned by Patrick Key). Jack recalls a prank he pulled on Ira - he tied a length of rope to the front door and secured it to the railings so Ira could not get out to do the milking at 5.00 a.m. one morning!

Ira used to take the train to Norwich every Saturday to visit "The Hills" (the livestock market in the centre of Norwich) to buy and sell cattle. He invariably came home slightly merry and his stockman Maurice Spooner (known as "Pin") would have done the milking. Quite often Ira would pay Maurice on the Saturday night, then forgetting, pay him again on the Sunday. "Pin" must have been delighted!

In the pair of semi-detached cottages opposite Cherry Tree there were two families. In the front cottage lived an ageing Mr. Waters (70) and his young wife (30) and to them was born one son, Bob Waters (known as "Bug").

In the other cottage lived a pair of bachelor brothers Harry & Joe Harboard. Harry was in the Navy for 25 years and served throughout the war. They were looked after by their sister, Hannah, who had a wooden leg. (They are buried in the churchyard).

The second dairy farm mentioned earlier was Marsh Farm where Charlie Brock (known as "Pom Pom") kept 6 cows and a bull called Tom. He was called Pom Pom because he used to sing to the cows "pom tiddely pom pom pom" as he milked them and if he stopped singing they stopped milking! This was in the early 1930's.

Charlie then moved into a property on Freethorpe Road. Next to Jack Wymers Bungalow stands another bungalow called "The Firs" where Chris and Kevin Thompson now live. Back in the 1930's there was a previous wooden building on this sight which Charlie & Anna Brock moved into. The chimney caught fire one day and it burnt down whilst they were out to tea and had to be rebuilt.

Charlie's son Alec Brock went on to work for the railway and was later farm manager at Sutton Farm, Freethorpe. Alec went on to have two daughters, one of whom, Ann Russell still lives in Limpenhoe today at "Oak Tree Cottage". Ann is the local Tree Warden. Her sister, Joy Brock lives in Freethorpe.
The family owned quite a lot of property and land in Limpenhoe.

Going back to Marsh Farm, when Charlie Brock left it was taken over by Bo Mallett - Bo then moved to a small holding in Brundall. It was then taken over by Lou and Sybil Edwards. They had been living in Reading Room Cottage (opposite the Rectory) and had three daughters, Maureen, Peggy and Audrey. Maureen went on to marry Nigel Key and is living at Southwood Hall. They had four children, three boys and a girl. Two of the boys, Patrick (known as "Pat") and Ben are farmers in Limpenhoe - one sheep and one cattle.

People had to make their own entertainment in those days. The train service was much more frequent, one every half hour to Gt. Yarmouth. A trip to the Regal Cinema and the last train home from Gt. Yarmouth at 11.30 p.m. was popular. Courting was carried out in Hobbs Lane (among other places). In those days Jack had an old motorbike for transport.

CANTLEY, LIMPENHOE & SOUTHWOOD REMEMBERED

The Falcon Pub was of course a great source of recreation and had a skittle alley in the outside building just inside the gate. Jack's Uncle Fred Wymer, who kept the pub for many years, also kept his chickens in this shed.

The landlord before Fred was Jimmy Lacey, who used to race around at 25 miles an hour in his Morris two seater car. Apparently his wife was not so keen on high speeds and would clutch her hat on shouting "no Jimmy, no, don't go so fast", whereupon Jimmy would give it another ten! That must have been a sight going through Thorpe St. Andrew on the outskirts of Norwich in 1938!

One additional attraction the pub offered was cold beer as they had a cellar. Jack maintains this was still one of the attractions in much later years. It was a Morgan Brewery tied house (long since swallowed up by one of the bigger breweries). After Fred left the pub the last landlord was Burgess. The pub closed in 1974.

During the war Jack remembers sheltering in the cellar. The bombs that fell on one occasion demolished a house on the hill and the blast also damaged the chapel, causing broken windows and damage to the roof – but there were no casualties. Since he was in a reserve occupation, all Jack's war years were spent in Limpenhoe. He says that no one went away to war from the village never to return.

Several planes came down in wartime. In February 1944 two B17's collided (due to low cloud) at the back of Reedham Hall, all 27 lives were lost. One plane was flown by Captain John Hutchinson - 550th Bomb Squadron, the other by 1st Lieutenant Warren Pease - 549th Bomb Squadron. An American bomber circled and crashed on the Halvergate marshes (this was dug up in about 1985).

A fighter plane came down on the East side of Limpenhoe Staithe and fortunately Jack's brother Alan Wymer and Nobby Carter were down there at the time and rescued the Canadian pilot by prising off the cockpit canopy with a handy bit of fencing.

Low Farm was farmed by Jack's father until his death in 1957. It had 55 acres of land (including about 20 acres of marsh) and 72 acres of Glebe land at the back of the village hall. Jack's mother, and brother, Roy, continued to live in the farmhouse until it was sold: the land having already been split up and sold.

There were other dwellings in Limpenhoe that have long since disappeared. Jack remembers his father talking about a property on what is now Maurice Moy's allotment (a corner of the field opposite Low Farm).

There were also two other properties on the Common. One was in the fleld (behind the signpost) opposite Cherry Tree Cottage. The original dwelling fell down and was replaced by a nissen hut. In the old dwelling lived "Frizzie" and the walk down to the marshes between this and Gandolph cottages was known as "Frizzies Wa1l". Likewise the walk down towards the factory was known as the "Chillico Wa1l".

The nissen hut was lived in by Mr. & Mrs. Rushmer (he was known as "Swalkie" - he liked the beer it seems). Jack used to act as Swalkie's clock and wake him up for work in the morning when he drove past. He did this by throwing stones on the nissen hut roof . Five children were raised by Swalkie and his wife in the early 1950's. One daughter, Kathy Rushmer, played darts for England. Freddie was the last one to leave and then the hut was removed.

Half way down the Chillico Wall just before Marsh Farm but on the opposite side was the Black Cottage - so named because it was tarred. The Sharman's lived there and Rosie Sharman is still alive today - although it is not known where she is living.

Gandolph Cottage's were three separate dwellings. In the first one lived Mr. and Mrs. George Canham (George was known as "Nigger") and was the local wart charmer until the late 1970's. They had two daughters Ida and Cynthia. Ida married an evacuee called Jimmy Hunt and they had one daughter Rosemary who is currently Landlady of the Red House at Cantley.

The last cottage was lived in by Mrs. Canham's father and a family called Merry lived in the middle cottage and their daughter Dawn is now living in Halvergate.

At the other end of the village, opposite the entrance to the Rectory was a tin church hall. This was used as a Mat Factory (made from Bull Rushes). The hut was moved from that sight into the farmyard and is the first tin shed in the corner of what is now Patrick Key's farmyard. The farmer at that time (Burton) used the shed as a potato store. Prior to Burton the land was owned by Bates.

Another thing which is gone but which Jack's father can remember is Limpenhoe Village Staithe. Wheat used to be taken down by horse and wagon and loaded into Wherries. On a Summer Sunday afternoon villagers would put on their best clothes and go and picnic on the grass round the staithe. (In the late 1970's Chris and Charlie Fisk tried to re-establish the rights for villagers to use the staithe as a mooring but were unable to get any agreement from the factory - whose Deeds will include the staithe records).

Limpenhoe Church Reverends were Rev. Housecroft; Rev. Gargery; Rev. Bevan; Rev. Thomas (who was a bit of a character) and Rev. Linden Ball. Rev. Ball was the last one to occupy the rectory and he is buried in the churchyard.

There is a photograph enclosed which shows the church before the new churchyard was added on. The first person to be buried in the new churchyard was Herbert Sales - he went everywhere with his bowler hat on and was laid to rest wearing it.

Peter recalls a conversation he had with the Rev. Linden Ball once when the Mallett Trust was mentioned. This was a sum of money left to the church by a wealthy patron from which the church got yearly interest – but this has now been wound up.

The church gate was paid for by Henry Preston but at the time of writing is in urgent need of replacement.

Jack Wymer and Peter Race. Photograph from Christine Fisk.

The late **Peter Race** - Was born in Billingford near Diss. His father worked at Southwood Hall Farm, then owned by Bob Key who was Uncle to Nigel Key Senior. Peter is not sure how long his father was there as he was very young at the time. He does however remember being at Limpenhoe School for a short time in 1929. He then went to live in Reedham in 1929 and apart from three years in the RAF lived there until he and Elsie were married on 17th May 1948 (They had their wedding reception in Cantley village hall) Like his father before him he then went to work at Southwood Hall Farm (he and Elsie lived in one of the farm cottages) until June 1955 when he decided to leave the land. He and Elsie moved to Limpenhoe and after a three month stint at a shop in Gt. Yarmouth, Peter went to work at the Cantley factory where he remained for 33 years until his retirement in September 1988. Their bungalow is between Low Farm and Cherry Tree Cottage. It was originally a prefab (owned by Alec Brock) which was bricked round. Peter and Elsie bought it in 1967.

Peter and Elsie had one son, John, who lives in Gorleston. He is a school teacher, married with two sons.

A quantity of photographs will also be found in the Time Capsule which Peter and Elsie have given.

Peter recalls many happy occasions in the Barn on the corner of Hobbs Lane, which was used by the Chapel for Anniversary's. Miss Nora Gotts from Cantley would play the organ and the children would say their pieces. These events raised money for the children's outings.

One snippet of information relating to the factory is that Ernie Pegg (known as "Snowball") laid the last brick that completed the building of the factory in 1912. He then went on to work there. It was a huge source of employment for all

the surrounding villages and shift workers were brought in by train and later by bus. A shift change involved up to 90 people in the 1960's (so much of the work being done by hand rather than machine) whereas today, it is about 12 or 13.
A further factory was built down by the river, the Chillico meat canning factory - it subsided quite soon after it was built!

On the day we wrote down all these memories (Saturday afternoon 30th January 1999) Jack and Peter had been to a funeral in the morning at Limpenhoe Church. Enos Carter (known as "Skipper" - and no relation of the other Limpenhoe Carter's) was buried. His mother and father had come here from South Africa and lived over the hill in the old part of the village. Enos married a local girl called Lucy. He and Jack were at school together and got up to all sorts of mischief by the sounds of things!
These notes were taken during three hours of conversation between Jack, Peter, Chris Thompson, and Charlie and Christine Fisk, all of Limpenhoe on Saturday 30th January 1999.

****

LIMPENHOE VOLES

The Limpenhoe Voles is a conservation group of volunteers of local residents. They were responsible in recent years for organising and fund raising for the restoration of the village hall, acquiring the playing field and planting trees and hedges along Hobbs Lane.
The adventure playground by the village hall was officially opened in August 2002 by Veronica Savage, and was followed by a fete.

Photograph on next page.
At the front: Sophie Flower.
Front Row from the left: Jacob Key, Melissa Key, William Key, Bradley Key, Sam Flower, Alex McNeil.
Middle Row: Thomas Chengvee, Joshua Chengvee, Jules Chengvee, Rosie Pearson, James Pearson, Alex Reader, Lorna's friend, Lorna Reader, Shane Key, Giles Leonard, Nigel Key, Brenda Pawsey.
Back Row: Wendy Figg, Hannah Pawsey, Ashley Howard, Nichola Bennett, Paul Collinson, Michelle Bennett, Gemma Powley, Hazel Leonard, Liza Howard, Richard Howard, Katherine Chengvee, Rory Reader.
Photograph supplied by Christine Fisk.

CANTLEY, LIMPENHOE & SOUTHWOOD REMEMBERED

Bottom: Limpenhoe Village Hall before restoration and rebuilding work was started in 2001, from Christine Fisk. Top: Local residents and the hedging plants in 1999, photograph by James Bass. 1900 shrubs and 50 trees were planted along a stretch of 600 metres. Some of the funding came from the Norfolk County Council Rural Action for the Environment.

Charles Fisk at the village Fete giving local children rides on the model steam engine tractor 'Hal', which he built as a 4" model of the Little Samson 5 ton tractor made by Savages of Kings Lynn in the early 1900s.. Supplied by Christine Fisk.

A RECENT POPULATION SURVEY

In March of 1999 Christine Fisk carried out a census of Limpenhoe and Southwood as part of the support for the Limpenhoe village hall refurbishment and to show the need for a playing field area.

The result showed that there were 45 dwellings in Limpenhoe, 9 dwellings in Southwood, and the total population was 160, of which 44 were children with an age of 16 or under.

She also recorded that there were 37 dogs, 19 horses and ponies and 1 donkey!

LIMPENHOE OCCUPATIONS FROM CENSUS RETURNS

The following table gives the occupations listed in some old census returns along with the number of people with the occupation. The largest number of workers was associated with agriculture in one way or another.

1861		1871		1891	
Agricultural lab	43	Annuitant	3	Agricultural Lab	6
Blacksmith	1	Butcher	1	Cook	2
Butcher	1	Carpenter	2	Cowkeeper /farmer	1
Carpenter	2	Car Woman	1	Domestic Servant	2
Charwoman	2	Dressmaker	2	Dressmaker	1
Chelsea Pensioner	1	Domestic Serv.	1	Farmer	7
Coal merchant	1	Farmer	4	Farmers Son	4
Cook	1	Gardener	1	Farm Manager	1
Cord-wainer	2	Innkeeper	1	Farm Labourer	23
Cowkeeper	2	Labourer	35	Grocer / Draper	1
Dressmaker	1	Land Steward	1	Groom	2
Farmer	6	Marsh Farmer	1	Groom / Gardiner	1
Groom/gardener	1	Marsh man	1	Housemaid	3
Housekeeper	1	Plate layer	2	Innkeeper	1
House servant	3	School mistress	1	Labourer	3
Innkeeper	1	Servant	2	Marsh Farmer	1
Marsh man	2	Shepherd	1	Marsh man	1
Medical Student	1	Shoemaker	2	Organist(?)	1
Pauper	4	Shop keeper	3	Pig dealer	2
Platelayer	1	Yeoman	1	Rate Collector	1
Rector	1			Rector	1
School mistress	2			Railway Signalman	1
Shoemaker	2			Railway Labourer	6
				Railway Platelayer	5
				School Mistress	1
				Shop Assistant	1
				Shepherd	1
				Smacksman	1

LIMPENHOE SURNAMES FROM CENSUS RETURNS

1861	1871	1881	1891
AYDEN	ALLEFLAK	AYDEN	BALEY
BALLS	AYDEN	BECK	BECK
BARKER	BARKER	BOSWELL	BOSWELL
BARNES	BECK	BULLARD	BOWEN
BECK	BENNS	BROWN	BULLARD
BLOGG	BIRD	CARTER	BROWN
BRANNON	BLYTH	CRISP	CARTER
BROWNING	BURNETT	CURTIS	CHURCH
CARVER	CALVER	DAY	CURTIS
CHESTER	CHESTER	DINGLE	DAY
CLARKE	CURTIS	DONELASS	DINGLE
COOPER	DINGLE	DOUGLASS	DUCKER
CULLUM	DOUGLAS	DUCKEY	DUGLAS
DINGLE	ETRIDGE	DUNHAM	EDWARD
DOUGLAS	FOWLER	ETTERIDGE	ELINGHAM
DRAKE	FUTTER	FOWLER	FEATHERS
ENGLAND	GRAY	FUTTER	FORDER
ETHERIDGE	HANTON	GADBOTH?	FOWLER
EVERITT	HARBORD	GADGE	FUTTER
FISK	HARRISON	GOWEN	GARWOOD
FOWLER	HOUSE	GRAY	GIBBS
GRAY	JACKSON	GRIFFON	GRAY
HADDON	JERMEY	GUNTON	HALL
HALL	KEY	HANTON	HARRISON
HAMMOND	LOADS	HARRIS	HAYWOOD
HANTON	MALE	HARRISON	HOWES
JACKSON	MALLETT	HOWARD	JACKSON
JERMYN	MOLL	JACKSON	JERMYN
KING	NEWMAN	JERMYN	KNIGHTS
LEATHES	NIKERSON	LAKE	LAKE
LEEDS	SAINT	LINFORD	LINFORD
LEMMON	SALES	LOADS	LOADS
LOADS	SCURL	MALLETT	MALLETT
MALE	SHEARING	MEAL	MEAL
MALLETT	SHEARMAN	MYHILL	MIMS
PLAFORD	SHREAVE	PEART	MOSS
RANDLE	SHORTEN	REMBLENCE	NICHOLS
ROSE	SIMMONDS	SALES	PEARCE
TOMPSON	SKIPPER	SHEARING	SALES
SADLER	TATE	SHORTON	SEAMAN
SALES	TURNER	SMITH	SEXTON
SEARLE	WARD	THIRKETTLE	SHEARING
SHEARING	WATERS	TURNER	SHORTEN
SHREEVE	WISEMAN	WARD	SISELAND
SHORTON		WATERS	SMITH
SKIPPER		WEBB	THURSTON
SPONER			TILLS
WATSON			WARD
WEBB			WATERS
			WEBB

1912 REGISTERED VOTERS FOR LIMPENHOE
Those marked with * are not resident in the parish.

Surname	First names	Qualifying property	
ALLEN	THOMAS PHILIP	COTTAGES ON COMMON	*
BAXTER	WILLIAM	BY NORWICH RD	
BECK	GEORGE	ON THE HILL	
BECK	WILLIAM	ON THE COMMON	
BRACEY	EDWARD	MARSHES	*
BRISTER	ALBERT	ON THE COMMON	
BROCK	CHARLES JAMES	ON THE COMMON	
BROCK	CHARLES JOHN	ON THE COMMON	*
BROWN	ARTHUR	BY NORWICH RD	
BROWN	MARTHA	ON THE COMMON	
BROWN	ROBERT	ON THE COMMON	
BROWNE	HENRY GEORGE	ON THE HILL	*
CARTER	ELIZABETH	BY THE CHURCH	
CARTER	HENRY	ON THE COMMON	
CARTER	WILLIAM	MARSHES	*
CURTIS	GEORGE FREDERICK	ON THE HILL	
CURTIS	WILLIAM	ON THE HILL	
DAY	THEODORE H. C.	NEAR CHURCH	*
EMERIS	WILLIAM CHARLES	HILL HOUSE FARM	*
FIELD	HERBERT EDWARD	OLD FALCON INN	
FOWLER	JOHN	ON THE COMMON	
FUTTER	WILLIAM	ON THE HILL	
GARWOOD	JOHN	ON THE COMMON	
GRAY	JOHN	ON THE COMMON	
HAYLETT	ROBERT	ON THE COMMON	
HEWITT	ISAAC WILLIAM	ON THE COMMON	
HEWITT	JAMES	BY RIVER	
HIGH	GEORGE HARDING	ON THE COMMON	*
HOUSECROFT	TOM	THE VICARAGE	
JERMYN	WILLIAM	ON HE HILL	
KEY	HENRY	BY OXPITS	*
KEY	ROBERT	ON THE COMMON	*
KEY	WILLIAM WESLEY	OXPITS	*
KEY	WALTER	ON THE HILL	*
LAKE	JAMES	BY NORWICH ROAD	
LINFORD	ETHELBERT	ON THE HILL	
LOADES	JOHN	ON THE HILL	
MALLETT	WILLIAM	ON THE COMMON	
MAY	ARTHUR JAMES	ON THE HILL	
MONSEY	ANNA ELIZABETH	LOW FARM	
NICHOLLS	WILLIAM senior	ON THE COMMON	
NICHOLLS	WILLIAM junior	ON THE HILL	
PRIOR	LEATHES	ON THE COMMON	*
ROSE	JAMES	ON THE HILL	

SALES	JOHN	ON THE HILL	
SALES	WILLIAM	ON THE COMMON	
SHARMAN	JOHN	MARSHES BY RIVER	*
SHEARING	ALBERT	MARSH FARM	
SMITH	JAMES	ON THE HILL	
SPOONER	JOHN	ON THE COMMON	
STONE	CHARLES	ON THE COMMON	
SUTTON	BENJAMIN CHARLES	MARSHES BY MILL	*
TILLS	HERBERT SAMUEL	BY THE CHURCH	
TURNER	BENJAMIN	ON THE HILL	
TURNER	GEORGE	ON THE HILL	
WALKER	JOHN	MARSH FARM	*
WATERS	HENRY JAMES	MARSHES	*
WATERS	HENRY LESLIE	ON THE COMMON	
WATERS	RALPH	MARSH	*

NAMES of LANDOWNERS on THE TITHE APPORTIONMENT of circa 1844.

AYERS, ANN BAKER, WILLIAM BROWN, HENRY BROWNING, HENRY NEGUS BURROUGHS, DANIEL COLLINS, FRANCIS DRAKE,OUGLAS, MICHAEL D REV. JOHN EMERIS, ROBERT GILBERT, WILLIAM HIGH, WILLIAM JERMYN, LEYTON'S DEVISEES, LIMPENHOE CHURCHWARDENS & OVERSEERS, DEVISEES OF BRUNNING MADDISON, JOHN MALLETT, SARAH MALLETT, WIDOW MILEHAM(?), LORD SIDNEY GODOLPHIN OSBORN, HENRY RUSHMER, THOMAS SCALES, MARGARET THIRKETTLE, RICHARD HENRY VADE WALPOLE, ANN WRIGHT, YARMOUTH & NORWICH RAILWAY CO., REV. JOHN JOHNSON (GLEBE), JOHN FRANCIS LEATHES.

SOUTHWOOD

The old Southwood parish was much smaller than Cantley and Limpenhoe in acreage, housing and population. It was, however, mentioned in the Domesday Book of 1086 which indicated that at that period of time it probably had a population similar to the population at Limpenhoe. The reason for the relative growth of Limpenhoe, and / or the decline in Southwood is unknown. It has been suggested that Southwood may have declined because of the plague of 1606, or simply because of a change in agricultural practices over the ages, but there is no definitive answer.

Today this old parish remains as an agricultural area with two farms.

The 1896 directory provides the following description:
"Southwood is a parish, about 1 ½ miles north from Cantley station on the Norwich and Lowestoft section of the Great Eastern railway, and 9 west from Yarmouth, in the Eastern division of the county, Blofield and Walsham petty sessional division,, hundred and union of Blofield, Yarmouth county court district, rural deanery of Blofield and archdeaconry and diocese of Norwich. The church of St. Edmund is in ruins. The inhabitants attend divine service at Limpenhoe. The register dates from the year 1675. The living is a discharged rectory consolidated with that of Limpenhoe, average tithe rent charge £210, joint net yearly value £156, including 10 acres of glebe. ..... H. R. Neville esq. is lord of the manor and chief landowner. The soil is light mixed; sub-soil, sand and gravel. The chief crops are wheat, barley and oats.
.... Letters through Norwich via Acle; Reedham is the nearest money order & telegraph office.
Pillar letter box, cleared at 8.20 am & 2.45pm weekdays only.
The children of this place attend the school at Limpenhoe"

FARMERS at SOUTHWOOD
The following people are found listed as farmers in the old directories and census returns.

Name	Dates listed	Notes
Samuel Walnes	1832 - 1845	Lived at property now known as 'Konigssee', but farmed land by Southwood House.
John Tuthill	1832 – 1865 (Died 1870)	Southwood Hall Farm, occupied 320 acres in 1845. Age 70 in 1861, farming 100 acres.
Elizabeth Maddison	1845 - 1861	Southwood House
William Case snr.	1854 – 1864 (Died 1868)	Age 59 in 1861, 505 acres, employing 11 men & 9 boys
William Case jnr.	1871 - 1883	Age 38 in 1871, 255acres.

George Burton	1871	Age 33 in 1871, 450 acres.
William Garrett	1881	Age 37 in 1881.
Mrs Caroline Garrett	1883	Wife of William.
Henry Bacon Riches	1888 – 1901 (Died 1909)	Age 37 in 1891. Hall Farm.
William Wesley Key	1891 -1912	Age 48 in 1891 at The Oaks but at the Hall by 1912.
John Key	1912	The Oaks
Robert Key	1922 - 1937	Hall Farm.
Arthur Marshland May	1922 - 1933	Oaks Farm.
Henry Preston	1937 – 1960s	The Oaks.

SOUTHWOOD HALL

The Hall is located at about TG39660543 and is mostly of 18th century build, but some parts are older and there are later additions. The hall is two storeys high with painted brick walls and has a slate roof. The associated buildings included a 2 storey high brick garden house with a thatched roof and some barns. One of the barns has a date stone of 1766.

The Hall was marked on Faden's Map as "Southwood Hall" and as 'Tuttles or Southwood House' on Bryant's Map.

On the 1845 tithe map of Southwood, the Hall is marked on area 17, and was occupied by farmer John Tuthill. The owners were listed as Richard H. Vade-Walpole and Reginald H. Neville.

John Tuthill occupied the farm for many years: he was listed in the 1832 voters register and in the 1865 directory

In July 1879 '**Southwood Farm**', which consisted of the Hall, the Summer House, coach house, stables and all the outbuildings along with eight cottages and 431 acres was put up for sale by auction. The farmhouse was described as having 4 attic rooms; six bedrooms, a nursery, apple room and water closet on the first floor, and on the ground floor: entrance hall, two staircases, dining room, drawing room, kitchen, gun-room, back kitchen, brew-house, dairy,, two store rooms, housemaids closet and a coal-cellar. The occupant at that time was farmer William Garrett who paid an annual rent of £750, and the owner Richard Walpole.

The farm was again put up for sale at the Royal Hotel in Norwich on 20th July 1907 .(NRO/BR184/2054) As Lot 1 in the sale it was described as "***The Hall Farm** Southwood. A freehold estate the farmhouse containing, on the Ground Floor: Entrance Hall, Dining Room, Drawing Room, Office, Kitchen, Back Kitchen, 2 Store Rooms, Housemaids Closet, Wine Cellar, 2 staircases. First Floor: 7 bedrooms and a WC. Upper floor: attics.*

Walled Gardens, Summer House, Range of outbuildings, Back Yard, Wash-House, Dairy,Coal & Wood House, Fowl's House, Riding Stables, Cow houses, 2 loose boxes, 3 stables, Harness Room. With extensive well arranged farm premises. Included in this lot was 407a 1r 37p and 3 cottages."
    Some past occupants include:
Henry Tuthill till about 1820, followed his son John Tuthill. William Garrett from 1876, then his widow Mrs Caroline Garrett was listed in 1883. Henry Bacon Riches was listed in 1888 and 1901. He married the widow Caroline Garrett. William Wesley Key, Robert Key and Nigel Key.
    In 1988 Nigel Key farmed about 500 acres and employed four men. The farm was mixed with about 100 sheep and 300 cattle, and grew sugarbeet, potatoes, peas, beans, wheat and barley.

The Southwood Hall Coronation Barn after conversion to a Celebration Venue

    In recent years the property has continued to be owned by the Key family and many of the outbuildings, including the grade II listed 'Coronation Barn', have been modified and converted to provide a Wedding and Events venue along with holiday accommodation.

SOUTHWOOD HOUSE / THE OAKS

Located on the Common at about TG397052
The house was shown on the tithe map on area 42, owned by John Emeris and occupied by Elizabeth Maddison. The associated farmland was occupied at that time by Samuel Walnes.
    A Mrs Maddison was listed living here at the house in the 1861 census as aged 76, a Land Proprietor.

The house here was marked on the 1880's O.S. map with the name 'SOUTHWOOD HOUSE' but later maps show the property here as 'THE OAKS'.
Some past occupants of the house and farm include:
William Wesley Key, followed by John Key, Arthur Marsland May, and Henry Preston.
   More recently the owner was Peter Key. Peter Key farmed about 270 acres rearing beef cattle and growing sugar-beet, wheat and barley.

ST EDMUNDS CHURCH, SOUTHWOOD.

The ruins of this church are located at about TG391053, covered by ivy and surrounded by scrub and hedge. It is a grade II listed building. On the Southwood tithe map and apportionment of 1845 the church is marked on area 25 which is listed as part of Southwood Glebe occupied by the farmer John Tuthill.
   The church was abandoned in about 1880 when Limpenhoe church was rebuilt. The church consisted of a rectangular west tower, chancel and nave, and was of flint with stone and brick dressing with a thatched roof.
   When the church was abandoned the church bell was removed to Limpenhoe, along with the 17th century Flemish tapestry depicting the sacrifice of Isaac by Abraham and a silver communion chalice bearing the words 'The towne of Southwood'.
   In the 1854 directory we have: "... *the living is a discharged rectory, valued in 1831 at £170, with the vicarage of Limpenhoe annexed to it. J. F. Leathes Esq.. is the patron; and the Rev. John Emenis, incumbent. The tithes are commuted for £145 per annum, and there are 7a of glebe. In 1801, the lord of the manor enclosed 6a of common land, and charged it with the payment of £4 yearly for the poor.*"
   The above mentioned lord of the manor in 1801 was Richard Walpole and the above £4 was to be paid by the occupant of the glebe to the minister, churchwarden and overseer to then be distributed to all the poor of the parish, whether resident or not, according to the number in the family, and at around Christmas time. In 1832 it is recorded that this "Poor's Rent" was distributed between 150 persons, a much higher figure than the population of Southwood at that time!
   White's 1864 directory provides the following brief description:
'*The Church is a plain whitewashed building, with nave, chancel, and square tower containing one bell. There is a triple lancet window at the east end, but the other windows are of the early decorated period. There are a piscina and an aumbry in the chancel, but the former is plastered over. Here is also a curious piece of tapestry representing Abraham offering up Isaac. The font is Norman, but disfigured with plaster and whitewash.*'
   Kelly's 1883 states:

'The church is a Gothic building, consisting of chancel, nave and plain square tower, but is now only used as a mortuary chapel. The inhabitants attend divine service at Limpenhoe. The register dates from the year 1675.'

The last marriage to take place at the church was on the 4th June 1878 between William Goffin and Sarah Elizabeth Webb, the service being conducted by the rector Rev. Day.

SOUTHWOOD CHURCH

Some Southwood Clergymen	Date
Roger Kynlet	
John de Fleming	1313
Richard de Dounton	1319
Thomas de Cleve	1323
John de Coliford.	1325
Walter de Bradford	1335
Roger Caly	
Stephen le Taliour	1357
Thomas de Dene	1389

John Benne	1391
John Waynhouse	1547
John Cullyner	c.1600
William Keen	1630
Edward Walters	1670
John Munnings Johnson	c.1845
John Emenis	c.1854

SOUTHWOOD CALLOW PIT LEGEND.

On the boundary of the parishes of Southwood and Moulton, is a pit called "Callow Pit". Once supposedly full of water but in dry summers now it is dry. Legend says that an iron chest, filled with gold, is engulfed in Callow Pit. Many years, ago two men, availing themselves of an unusually low state of the water, decided to get the treasure. Having formed a platform of ladders across the pit, they inserted a staff through the ring in the lid of the chest, and raised it up from the waters, and placed the staff on their shoulders, ready to take their prize on their temporary bridge. One of the men triumphantly exclaimed: 'We've got it safe, and the devil himself can't get it from us.' Instantly the pit was enveloped in a cloud of steam, with a strong sulphurous smell; and a black hand and arm emerged from the water, and grabbed the chest. A struggle ensued and the chest, with the treasure, sank beneath the water, never to be seen again. The men carried off only the ring from the chest lid which they placed on Southwood Church door! This ring was later taken to Limpenhoe church.

REFLECTIONS ON SOUTHWOOD by BRENDA AND PAUL PAWSEY.

In November 1985 we moved from our cosy, modern centrally heated bungalow in Wickhampton to live at White House Cottages, Church Road in Southwood. These were a pair of farm-workers' tied houses previously owned by Henry Preston at Oaks Farm and described as "in need of restoration".

It was one of the coldest nights of that winter – the temperature dropped to minus 11 degrees centigrade – with as much ice on the inside of the metal windows as on the outside. We huddled around one tiny open fire with several layers of clothes on surrounded by boxes and furniture. Not the warmest of welcomes to our new home!

One cottage was almost derelict and had not been lived in for several years. The other had been modestly modernised but had stood empty for almost a year. We set about converting them into our home now known as 'Konigssee' using recycled traditional materials whenever possible to retain the character of the property.

And so our new family lifestyle of self-sufficiency, organic gardening and growing fruit and vegetables, and alternative energy living began. A wonderful, isolated, rural location with natural surroundings full of wildlife – ideal for bringing up our two daughters Emma-Kate and Hannah-Jane.

This "good life" did have problems though. Getting snowed-in during severe winters. Once for six days. Endless electricity power failures due to the overhead cables being affected by adverse weather conditions. This led to Paul designing and self building a wind turbine from all scrap materials to generate some of our own electricity in 1998. Sadly the 1987 October "hurricane" uprooted our magnificent seventy foot high mature Elm tree which was still in full leaf. A great loss as it was one of the few remaining examples in this area unaffected by Dutch Elm disease.

During their schooldays at Acle High School our girls were encouraged to research their village history as part of the curriculum. This we did with great interest and enthusiasm, especially the Callow Pit Coffer legend, St. Edmunds ruined church, the reasons for the village decline due to a disastrous flood followed by a deadly plague in 1606, and the history of the farming families and local community. Members of the South and Wright families who had previously lived here visited from time to time and were keen to see the house alterations and conversion in progress. They recalled and remembered how things had been during their lifetime. We have traced maps back to the 18th century which shows a small farmhouse on this site together with a 100 apple tree orchard which was ploughed up in the late 1950s. We have reinstated an orchard but with just 10 fruit trees.

Pre 1st World War records show that then there were 5 more cottages in the neighbouring fields where members of the Brister, Carr, Curtis, Jermy, Rope and Rose families lived.

In 1881 there were 44 residents recorded. Now in 2014 there is 12 plus 1 child!

Southwood has sometimes been referred to as "a vanishing village of Norfolk" and not easy to find.

The trouble is knowing when you are in it and realising it before you are out of it again!

It consists of two farms, a ruined church and a few cottages. Recently, however, a converted barn complex now hosts a wedding venue.

Our only public amenity is a Victorian post box and a small triangular grass area where a tree was planted in memory of Princess Diana at the bottom of Oaks Lane.

So although Southwood has been "tiny" in all the days of living memory and was described as "fading away" in the 1950s – IT AIN'T GONE YET!

Konigssee in Spring of 1986 undergoing renovation. The Elm tree in the background was uprooted in the gale of 1987. Photograph supplied by Paul & Brenda Pawsey.

Some past occupants at the two cottages, now known as Konigssee, include:
Mr & Mrs Brinded in the 1920s, the Wright family from 1930 to 1939, Patterson family 1939 to 1944, South family 1945 to about 1978, Wade in the early 1980s.
The second cottage had the Balls family from 1930 to 1932, Edwards family 1932 to 1939 and the Wright family from 1939 till 1982.

CANTLEY, LIMPENHOE & SOUTHWOOD REMEMBERED

SOUTHWOOD OCCUPATIONS FROM CENSUS RETURNS

1861		1871		1891	
Agricultural Lab	7	Ag Labourer	8	Ag Labourer	7
Carter	1	Cook	1	Cook	1
Dairymaid	1	Domestic servant	3	Domestic servant	1
Farmer	2	Farmer	2	Farmer	2
Gardner	2	Farm Servant	1	Farm Bailiff	1
Groom	1	Farm Bailiff	1	Governess	1
House servant	4	Governess	1	Housemaid	1
Housemaid	1	Groom	1	Nursemaid	1
Land Proprietor	1	Hawker	1	Shepherd (retired)	1
		Laundress	1		
		Pauper	1		

SOUTHWOOD SURNAMES FROM CENSUS RETURNS

1861	1871	1881	1891
BONE	BOX	BOATWRIGHT	BAILEY
BUNN	BURTON	CARR	CALVER
CARR	CARR	CARTER	CHANEY
CASE	CASE	CASE	ELLENSHAW
GREEN	DONGELL	FOSTER	GARRETT
GODBOLT	GODBOLT	GARRETT	HARDESTY
HAIFH	GROOM	HOOD	JERMY
HOOKER	HARPER	HOWES	KEY
HOWES	LANN?	PORTER	KIRK
JONES	MATHEWS	RUSHMER	MYHILL
MADDISON	TURNER	SHARMAN	PLUMMER
RUSHBROOK	WARD	TAYLOR	RICHES
TURNER	WEBB	TURNER	TURNER
TUTHILL		WALLER	WEBB
WARD		WANT	
WYMER		WEBB	

1912 REGISTERED VOTERS FOR SOUTHWOOD

Surname	First Names	Qualifying Property	
CURTIS	HENRY	LIMPENHOE RD	
FUTTER	WILLIAM	FREETHORPE RD	
KEY	JOHN	THE OAKS	
KEY	WILLIAM WESLEY	THE HALL	
TOVELL	SAMUEL	FREETHORPE RD	
TURNER	FRED	LIMPENHOE RD	
TURNER	JAMES	FREETHORPE RD	
WEBB	CHARLES	LIMPENHOE RD	
WYMER	DENNIS	LIMPENHOE RD	

POPULATION FROM CENSUS RETURNS.

Censuses were taken every ten years and gave the number of inhabitants and the number of houses in each parish. The table here shows the population for each of the three parishes as male (M), female (F) and total (T).

In March of 1884 the detached part of Southwood was amalgamated with Limpenhoe. The detached Southwood was close to the river and was marshland which was unpopulated.

The following tables show that the population of Southwood changed very little throughout the twentieth century; on the other hand housing and population at Cantley is seen to increase significantly in the 1920s following the alterations at the Cantley Sugar factory.

In 1935 the civil parishes of Southwood and Limpenhoe were incorporated into Cantley, while the detached part of Cantley was amalgamated with the enlarged Halvergate parish.

YEAR	CANTLEY			LIMPENHOE			SOUTHWOOD		
	M	F	T	M	F	T	M	F	T
1801	135	112	247	54	41	95	28	14	42
1811	115	107	222	59	53	112	15	15	30
1821	131	120	251	70	72	142	25	15	40
1831	153	112	265	81	75	156	25	29	54
1841	110	100	210	94	92	186	26	26	52
1851	140	137	277	121	127	248	22	26	48
1861	120	114	234	117	110	227	18	21	39
1871	129	120	249	101	92	193	25	22	47
1881	134	132	266	100	99	199	18	26	44
1891	131	126	257	101	103	204	26	28	54
1901	148	122	270	86	102	188	25	29	54
1911	130	129	259	71	82	153	24	23	47
1921	149	142	291	83	93	176	16	21	37
1931	208	198	406	77	79	156	23	17	40
1951	270	283	553	Limpenhoe and Southwood were incorporated into Cantley following the Norfolk Review of 1935.					
1961	269	253	522						
1991			676						
2001			677						
2011									

HOUSES

The following table shows the number of dwellings in the three parishes according to the census returns.

YEAR	CANTLEY	LIMPENHOE	SOUTHWOOD
1801	39	24	-
1811	48	18	-
1821	37	21	-
1831	38	35	6
1841	46	38	9
1851	54	49	9
1861	49	48	9
1871	54	47	10
1881	54	44	10
1891	53	45	10
1901	54	47	11
1911	61	45	11
1921	66	40	11
1931	100	42	11
1951	168	Limpenhoe and Southwood were incorporated into Cantley following the Norfolk Review of 1935.	
1961	179		
2001	279		

AREAS

The table shows the acreage of the three parishes from past records.

YEAR	CANTLEY	LIMPENHOE	SOUTHWOOD
1831	2970	940	350
1841	1788	1010	471
1851	1850	1075	481
1881	1850	1075	481
1891	1847	1128	439
1931	1847	1127	439
1951	3191	Incorporated into Cantley.	

The CANTLEY Tithe Map and Apportionment of circa 1837 says the total area of the roads, waters, half of the river, river walls and drains comes to 62a 3r 13p. New apportionments were issued for Cantley first in 1847 following the Norfolk Railway Company acquiring some of the land, again in 1921 after Norfolk County Council acquire some land, and later in 1930 to show the land taken over by the newly formed East Anglian Real Property Company Ltd. East Anglian Real Property Co Ltd. owned 792a 0r 26p at that time, and the Sugar Beet Corporation owned 32a 2r 16p.

The LIMPENHOE Tithe Map and Apportionment of circa 1845 gives the following information: areas of 1043a 1r 23p, Mill drains of 1a 6p, roads of 7a 1r 2p, river 16a 2r 20p, and roads of 7a 1r 2p giving a total of 1075a 19p.

On the SOUTHWOOD Tithe Map and Apportionment of 1845 we have; 372a 36p arable, 98a 2r 24p meadow & pasture, 6a 1r 21p of roads, and 4a 2r 16p of river giving a total of 481a 3r 17p.

The three parishes belonged to the Blofield Union from 1834, when the Blofield Poor Law Union was formed, until 1930 when the Union was dissolved. Prior to that time the parishes were in the Acle Gilbert Union which was formed in 1788.

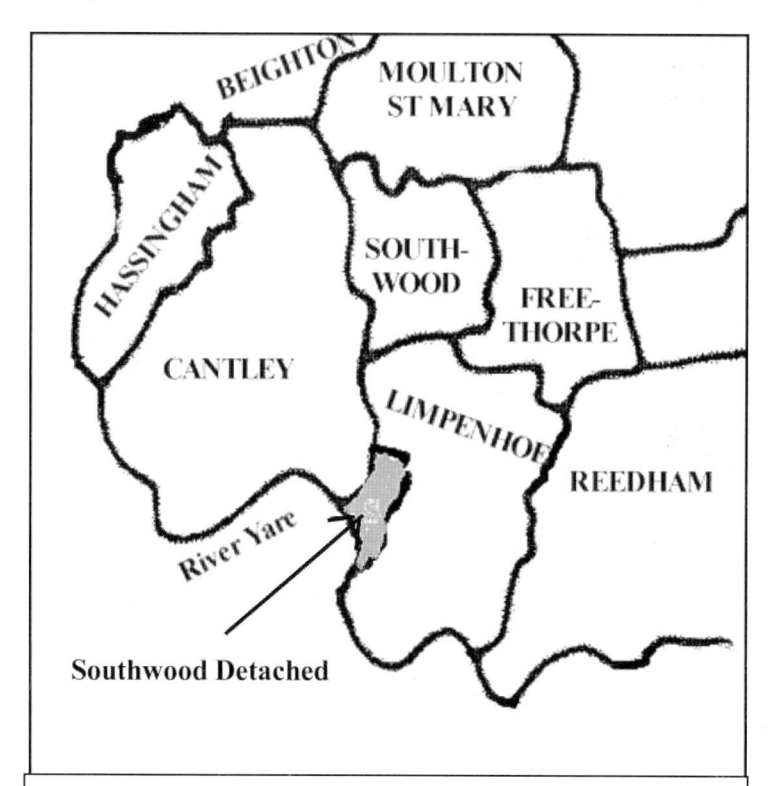

The civil parishes of Cantley, Limpenhoe and Southwood as they appeared prior to 1884, when the detached portion of Southwood adjacent to the River Yare was incorporated into Limpenhoe. The detached Cantley is not shown on this map as it was adjacent to the River Bure.

EARLIER DAYS

A Neolithic adze is the earliest datable artefact to have been found in the parish close to the River Yare. A flint flake of prehistoric date has also been discovered in the village.
     Several ring ditches have been recorded in the parish that are believed to be the remains of Bronze Age barrows.
     Cropmarks are visible in the parish and may be a settlement or enclosure of late Iron Age or Roman date. Roman objects have been found and a rectangular enclosure has been recorded that may be a Roman farmstead.

From the Domesday Book:
In the Domesday Book Cantley was held by King William I, who also held part of Limpenhoe. William of Ecouis held part of Limpenhoe and part of Southwood. The last part of Limpenhoe was in the annexation of Baynard, as was part of Southwood. The remaining two sections of Southwood were held by Godric the Steward and Ralph Baynard.

Cantley
58 households, 4 villagers, 42 smallholders, 2 slaves, 10 freemen, 2 lord's plough teams, 10 men's plough teams, 44 acres of meadow, 60 woodland pigs, 1 salthouse, 400 sheep, 1 cobs and 6 pigs.

Limpenhoe
30 households, 20 freemen, 3 men's plough teams and 78 acres of meadow.

Southwood
31.5 households, 26 freemen, 2 smallholders, 2 plough teams, and 2 acres of meadow.

POSSIBLE ORIGIN OF NAMES

Cantley is from old English " Canta + Leah" meaning Canta's clearing.

Limpenhoe is from old English "Limpa + hoh" meaning Limpa's Hill-spur.

Southwood is from "Suth + Wald" meaning Southern Wood.

LISTED BUILDINGS

The following information from www.britishlistedbuildings.co.uk shows the listed buildings in the current Civil Parish of Cantley.

Barn 200 Metres SE of Southwood Hall, Grade II, The Common. TG39710535.

Barn 3 Metres NW of Southwood Hall, Grade II, Southwood. YG39650548.

Church of St Botolph, Grade II, Church Road, Limpenhoe. TG 39530399.

Church of St Margaret, Grade II, 62 Church Road, Cantley. TG38170414.

Garden House and Attached Garden Walls, 60 M NE of Southwood Hall, Grade II, The Common, Southwood. TG39700542.

Remains of Church of St Edmunds, Grade II, Norwich Road, Cantley. TG39110532.

Southwood Hall, Grade II, The Common, Southwood. TG39660543.

Tombstone 20 Cm West of St Margaret's Church Adjacent to North Tower Corner Grade II, 62 Church Road, Cantley. TG38150414.

Tombstone 20 Cm West of St Margaret's Church Adjacent to South Tower Corner Grade II, 62 Church Road, Cantley. TG38105414

Tombstone 7 Cm to North of West Tower of Church of St Botolph, 13th Century coffin. Grade II, Church Road, Limpenhoe. TG 39510399.

REFERENCES AND BIBLIOGRAPHY

The River Yare: Breydon & Beyond, 9780954168377, Sheila Hutchinson, 2010.
The Lower Bure from Great Yarmouth to Upton, 97809654168360, Sheila Hutchinson, 2008.
A History of the Royal Norfolk & Suffolk Yacht Club, Jamie Campbell, 9780903094108, 2009.
Census Returns for Cantley, Limpenhoe & Southwood for 1841, 1851, 1861, 1871, 1881, 1891, 1901 at Norfolk Libraries, and 1911 on the internet.
Various old Norfolk Directories from 1836 to 1937.
Cantley, Limpenhoe & Southwood Tithe Maps and Apportionments on micro-film at Norfolk Records Office.
Licence Registers PS8/6/1-4 at Norfolk Records Office.
Websites with useful information include:
www.familysearch.org
www.historic-maps.norfolk.gov.uk
www.old-maps.co.uk
www.domesdaymap.co.uk
www.cantley.org
www.cantley.norfolk.sch.uk

Other books by Sheila Hutchinson:

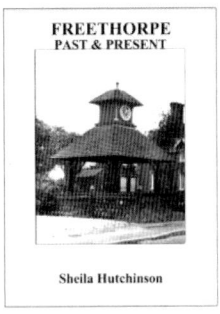

- BERNEY ARMS PAST & PRESENT
- THE HALVERGATE FLEET: PAST & PRESENT
- THE ISLAND (THE HADDISCOE ISLAND) PAST & PRESENT
- BERNEY ARMS REMEMBERED
- BURGH CASTLE REMEMBERED
- REEDHAM REMEMBERED
- REEDHAM MEMORIES
- THE LOWER BURE FROM GREAT YARMOUTH TO UPTON
- THE RIVER YARE: BREYDON & BEYOND
- FREETHORPE PAST & PRESENT
- WICKHAMPTON MEMORIES
- HALVERGATE & TUNSTALL REMEMBERED